Not only in Indian history but in the international history also Shivaji's personality is uncomparable and extraordinary. His life was an ideal combination of many virtues like understanding, dutifulness, good character, communal harmony etc. A complete assessment of Shivaji's character and works can be a topic for research.

Shivaji was the son of a simple *jagirdar*. He became the founder of the Maratha empire on his own strength. He added a new chapter in history and started a new age. Light is being thrown here on his virtues in brief.

Chhatrapati Shivaji

Bhawan Singh Rana

DIAMOND BOOKS

Publisher : **Diamond Pocket Books (P) Ltd.**
X-30, Okhla Industrial Area, Phase-II
New Delhi-110020
Phone : 011-40712200
E-mail : sales@dpb.in
Website : www.diamondbook.in

Chhatrapati Shivaji
By - *Bhawan Singh Rana*

Contents

Preface

The name of epoch-maker Chhatrapati Shivaji is not unknown to any Indian. He added a new chapter to history by establishing an independent Hindu state at the time when the entire country was under Muslim rule. He proved that the soul of the Hindu has not slept yet by his successful effort. No Hindu had done such praiseworthy work for centuries. His deeds become more important because he was the son of an abandoned woman. His father gave no contribution to his life. His father, Shahji, performed his last duty by giving him the *Jagir* of Poona under the custodianship of Mata Jijabai and Dadaji Konddeo. As a result he did not get proper education, even then he established an independent state with his own strength. In fact a lion is not coronated. He occupies the status of *Vanraj* (king of jungle) with his own strength.

The virtues like unique political wisdom, unique cleverness, extraordinary courage, praiseworthy character etc. are other qualities of Shivaji's personality. Despite having the utmost faith in his religion, culture and nation, he had goodwill and respect for all other religions and communities. There was no room for religious or castewise discrimination in his politics. Many western critics have also praised him. His ideals are timely for our present nationalism. This is the aim of this book.

The books by famous historians Sir Yadunath Sarkar, Govind Sakharam Sardesai and James Grand Dough have been consulted while writing this book. The contents of this book are completely in accordance with history. The disputed contents have properly been mentioned.

Bhawan Singh Rana

One

Family Introduction and Early Life

Family Tradition

There are a few in the world who get name and fame on the basis of their families, but there are some others also who brighten the name of their families with their own deeds. Chhatrapati Maharaj Shivaji was a person of the second type. He was a descendant of the Bhosle family. Even the historians are in doubt about the origin of the Bhosle family, but the Bhosles claim themselves to be the descendants of the Sisodiya dynasty of Mewar. It is said that Banvir had fled away to the south when Maharana Udai Singh had ascended to the throne of Chittor (Banvir was the then king of Chittor who had tried to kill Udai Singh in his childhood, but thanks to Panna Dhay who sacrificed her own son and saved the child Udai Singh). He was the son of Maharana Sanga's brother from a maidservant and it is said that Bhosles were his descendants in Maharashtra. Another belief is that Alauddin Khilji had capured Chittor in 1303. One of the kins of the then royal family, Sujan Singh or Sajjan Singh had fled away to the south. He had died around 1350. Ugrasen was born in the fifth generation after him who had two sons, Karna Singh and Shubhkrishna. Karna Singh's son Bhim Singh was given the title of 'Raja Ghorpade Bahadur' by the Bahmani King. The descendants of Bhim Singh are called the 'Ghorpade' and those of Shubhkrishna are called the Bhosle.

Babaji Bhosle was the grandson of Shubhkrishna who had died in 1597. Babaji Bhosle had two sons, Maloji and

Bithoji. It is said that these two had such healthy and gigantic bodies that even horses could not even carry them. They were the bodyguards of Lukji Jadhavrao, the chief of Sindkheda and were the Patils of a village near Daulatabad. Daulatabad became the capital of the Nizamshahi kingdom after the decline of Ahmed Nagar kingdom. Lukji Jadhavrao became a chieftain of the highest order under this dynasty. It should be noted that Lukji Jadhavrao was the descendant of the 'Yadav Dynasty' of Devgiri. Maloji and Bithoji began to arrange for their paternal land working under Lukji Jadhavrao.

Shahji Bhonsle

Shahji was the elder son of Maloji and Sharifji was the younger. Once Maloji alongwith Shahji went to Lukji Jadhavrao's place as an invitee on the occasion of either 'Holi' or 'Vasant Panchami'. People were pouring colour on each other gaily. Jijabai, the daughter of Lukji Jadhavrao, was sitting with Shahji and was of the same age. Seeing the elders enjoying with colours, these two also started pouring colour on each other. When Lukji Jadhavrao looked at the innocent amusement of the children he uttered suddenly, "What a beautiful couple these two look like!"

Maloji at once announced in a loud tone, "Look all! You are eyewitnesses, Lukji Jadhavrao has fixed the engagement of his daughter with my son."

Lukji Jadhavrao opposed Maloji's statement severely. He told that he had not spoken those words intentionally. In fact Maloji was only a servant to Lukji Jadhavrao. How could he give his daughter in marriage to a servant's son? A conflict rose between them on this issue and Maloji resigned from his service. He then started working to raise his status. He developed a strong relationship with Mallick Amber, the military chief of Nizamshah. A little later Nizamshah of Ahmed Nagar gave him the charge of five thousand horses and the title of 'Raja Bhonsle'. The forts of Shivneri and Chakan came under his control. He also got the '*Jagirs*' of Poona and Supe. Later, Nizamshah on the insistence of Mallick Amber, made Lukji Jadhavrao agreeable for the marriage of Shahji and Jijabai. Ultimately they were married in November 1605. Later this dramatically combined couple became the source of the birth of Chhatrapati, the creator of history.

Birth and Childhood of Shivaji

The historians are not unanimous on the date of Shivaji's birth. One opinion is that he was born from the womb of Jijabai on the 2nd day of the light half of 'Vaisakh' of 1549 Shak Samwat (Thursday, the 6th of April 1627) in the fort of Shivner. Another thought says that it was the 3rd day of the dark half of Falgun 1551 Shak Samwat (Friday, the 19th of February 1630). There is a difference of almost three years between these two dates but it makes no difference to the greatness of Shivaji.

Jijabai gave birth to six sons including Shivaji. Unfortunately four of them died in the early age. The elder of the remaining two was Sambhaji. Probably he was born in 1616.

Shivaji's childhood was not at all happy. He didn't even get his father's protection for long. Hence, the foundation of an independent empire is undoubtedly a surprise in such adverse situations. The two great persons behind this surprise were mother Jijabai and Dadaji Konddeo. The life of Shivaji got root in childhood under the supervision of these two guides.

The Patronage of Jijabai

Jijabai was the daughter of Lukji Jadhavrao. Her arteries carried the blood of the Yadav rulers of Devgiri. Her marital life was not a happy one. It was almost the life of a divorced woman (abandoned woman). Jijabai and Shahji had nearly become the two opposite banks of a river when Shivaji was in her womb. Shahji married Tukabai, a girl from the Mohite family of Supa. Jijabai started living with Konddeo who was the caretaker of Shahji's *jageer* of Poona.

Her elder son, Sambhaji, lived with his father. The famous historian, Govind Sakharam Sardesai, has written about Jijabai's condition a few days before the birth of Shivaji: "Who would guide her that she should have gone to her fahter-in-law's house and asked him for her lookafter? She didn't get a chance of face-to-face meeting with her husband. If, by chance, it happened, she didn't have the courage to discuss her condition. Shahji rode away after impregnating Jijabai. Hence, the in-laws had to care for her. We can't ignore this famous tale." Jadhavrao incidentally met Jijabai on the way near Junnar when he was returning from Shahji. That time she had a pregnancy of seven months. Jadhavrao tried to send her to Sindkheda. What a difficult situation it was! Nobody is greater than the husband for an Arya woman. Even if the husband had abandoned her, she did not agree to her father's offer. She went to the fort of Shivner which was nearby and under the control of the Bhonsle. There she gave birth to Shivaji. The elder one, Sambhaji, started helping his father. He began to learn philosophies of life, state affairs, warfare, etc. from his father. Sambhaji never remembered his mother.

Brutal Assassination of Lukji Jadhavrao

Earlier Lukji Jadhavrao was the chieftain of Nizamshah, but later he gave up this post and went into the service of the Mughal emperor Shahjehan. He worked for the Mughal emperor living in Sindkhera. Nizamshah could not tolerate this. Lukji pinched the Nizam like a thorn. He summoned all the Jadhav chiefs to Daulatabad for a meet on the 25th of July, 1629. None could have even imagined that he would stab in the back. Jadhavrao along with his sons, grandson and many Jadhav chiefs reached there. Most of them had been slaughtered there mercilessly. Lukji Jadhavrao, his sons Achaloji and Raghuji and his grandson Yashwantrao had to lose their lives.

Jijabai could not forget this inhuman infidelity to her father, brothers and the nephew throughout her life. Perhaps the sense of revenge originated due to this incident and she vowed to destroy the Mohammadan which resulted in the emergence of Shivaji, the founder of an era.

Secret Dwelling of Child Shivaji

Shahji along with Mallick Amber had been fighting against the Mughals for many years before this incident. The Mughal emperor tried a lot to capture Shahji and his family after they had occupied (captured) the fort of Daulatabad. Jijabai was living with Shivaji in the fort of Shivner. Mahadal Khan, chief of the Mughal emperor came over to the fort to capture them. Jijabai knew Mahadal Khan so she sent him a message that she herself would see him and he waited for her being assured. First Jijabai sent Shivaji alongwith a faithful maid to an unknown place and then went to Mahadal

Khan where she was made a captive. Shivaji lived with the same maid, whom he used to call *Dhay ma*, for two years. Luckily Jijabai got free and again concentrated on the look-after of her son.

The place where Shivaji was kept hidden is called Shivapur or Kher-Shivapur. This falls on the way from Poona to Satara. Jijabai named it Shivapur after the name of her son. There was some paternal land of the Bhonsle on which Jijabai had developed the 'Shahbag' or 'Shahgarden', a mango orchard.

Jijabai faced all these hardships with determination. She had neither money, custodian nor servants at the time of Shivaji's birth. She had left her father and had come to the fort of Shivner to live with her husband, but he too went to the battlefield leaving her alone. After some time she left the fort of Shivner and went into the fort of Osad. She took the temple of goddess Shivai in the fort to be the hermitage in this disappointing situation. She had lost four of her sons earlier, so she kept on praying goddess Shivai day and night for the long life of Shivaji. Still she never tried to create any nuisance to the relation of her husband with his co-wife even if she was in such terrible conditions.

Departure to Poona

Shahji was fighting for Nizamshah against the Mughals at the time of Shivaji's birth. Shahjehan himself went to the Deccan in January 1636. Thc Nizamshahi had come to an end by then. A treaty was signed between the Bijapur sultanate and the Mughal emperor in May 1636. After this Shahji went into the service of Bijapur. He had been rewarded a land piece (*jagir*) to the south of the Godavari river in return for his services. It had happened in October 1636. Shahji had retained his hold over the property (*jagir*) of Poona even in these years of struggle. He appointed some faithful people to take care of his new *Jagir* and went to Bijapur.

Shahji had sent Jijabai and Shivaji to Poona before he left for Bijapur. He had appointed a very efficient person, Dadaji Konddeo, as the caretaker of his *Jagir* of Poona. Shivaji had been about seven-eight years by this time. This was the first happy incident in Shivaji's life. His life had been a life of misery prior to this. Though chaotic and scattered, but at least he had become the owner of a property (*Jagir*). Above all, he had a very good and competent guide in Dadaji Konddeo.

Under the Supervision of Dadaji Konddeo

The first man, child Shivaji found as his custodian, was Dadaji Konddeo. In fact he only laid down the foundation of Shivaji's life. His life before this had been a savage one. He started his new life under the guardianship of Dadaji Konddeo, who was a Brahmin from Malthan. He had other surnames also such as Gochiwadi, Hokar, Parnekar, Malthankar etc. Earlier he was in the service of the ruler of Bijapur. Later he received training in warfare from Mallick Ambar. He had helped Shahji in the battle against the Mughal emperor.

Dadaji Konddeo took Jijabai and Shivaji to Poona in Sept-Oct 1636. He was the manager of this state of Shahji now. He maintained his responsibilities here with such love and honesty that it not only became a praiseworthy one but also an example for others. His contributions towards making Shivaji the founder of a Hindu state are uncomparable.

Dadaji Konddeo paid the maximum attention to agricultural development as soon as he took charge of the state. Lawlessness had spread all around the state then and hence it was his prime duty to eliminate it and establish a good law and order system in the state. He employed officers to manage villages and corrected the condition of revenue. For the first five years the farmers were exempted from paying any revenue. He also tried to increase the agricultural production Murar Jagdeo had ploughed these fields with asses. He used a golden plough and kicked off agriculture to end up the ill-effect of ass-ploughing. Efficient farmers were inhabited there calling from outside. Dadaji Konddeo did all this living in Poona; hence first of all he built a better residence with a beautiful garden. Shivaji had lived here only during his secret dwelling.

Shivaji also felt the disarray of his state. One day he asked his mother, "Why is such lawlessness in the state? Why do you always look worried and nervous? Tell me which work of yours I can do. Even if I am young, I can at least do small jobs." Jijabai had her throat choked with emotion at the child's feelings. She could not make any reply. She told Dadaji

Konddeo, "You only can make reply to Shiva's questions. It will be better if he has everything clear in his mind. What are we, what is our status today and how will the things maintained in future? You have to make all this clear to him as Shahji has left him under your guidance."

Dadaji Konddeo, like a very efficient custodian, told everything to Shivaji in a very easy language which meant as follows:

"Raje (nick name)! You are young now. You don't know about your status today. You are the son of the brave Shahji Raja who had to go away to far off place in order to save his life. I, you, your mother all are in exile now. We don't have even a better place to live in. The Mughal emperor has dethroned us seven years ago. Shahji Raja could not resist the strong Mughal army. It is enough that he could safely get away. I have been serving under Shahji Raja for the last fifteen years and now our future rise depends completely upon your leadership. My body had developed under his patronage only. Our paternal state Poona has almost been shattered. We will be in a better condition only if it is corrected. We have been running through difficulties for quite a few years. Mohammadans have caused devastation everywhere. They cheated the valiant commander Jadhavrao. They called him for a meeting and killed him. The mother of Shahji was from the Nimbalkar family. Her brother, Bajaji Nimbalkar, took charge of the Phalpatan estate. The Shah of Bijapur called him for a meeting and changed his religion. Today he is living in Bijapur as an irreligious person. What an irony it is! It is the mercy of God that your mother has not faced such irony."

These words created a cyclone of thoughts in Shivaji. He became very eager to take revenge for these atrocities. There occurred a revolutionary change in his thoughts. He became fully dedicated for the foundation of self-religion and self-government. His determination resulted in making him Chhatrapati Shivaji. First of all he removed the lawlessness from his state and made it into a well-managed one. He then formed a group of people of the same ideology as his. Mata Jijabai and Dadaji Konddeo became his advisors and guides.

The Poona estate was comprised of only 24 regions. 12 out of them were in Mawal and Junnar and the remaining 12 were under Poona. The word *Nawal* means the land situated at the banks of a small river flowing between two hills. There was a work agent and an accountant Deshpandey in every Mawal. Shivaji also lived in a Mawal during his secret dwelling. He had roamed a lot in the stretches of this 150 miles long and 30 miles wide uneven territory, hence he was well acquainted with its nooks and corners. The benefit that Shivaji got by living in this area was that he had a very good practice of moving in such arduous areas where he was now moving for his estate purposes. An eyewitness has written in this regard:

"I have been watching Shivaji's activities very closely for the last eight years. There is no limit of his wits and expeditions. He is frequently visiting villages day and night. He never cares for sun, rain, hunger, thirst etc. He goes to any hut and asks for food and spends the night there. He meets people, asks them questions, extracts important information from them and discriminating between just and unjust knows everything. It is beyond calculation how many days he has spent wandering like this. He remained out of his house even for months. The poor mother remained worrying at home about his whereabouts and also for his well-being. When he returns home after a long gap, he explains all his experiences to his mother. This raises the mother's curiosity. He tells her how the Muslim officers loot the people, demolish the temples, forcibly take away the Hindu women and don't even care for just or unjust. He sees all these activities with his eyes and consoles people. He also provokes them to fight against these. People gather around him to listen to his thoughts. He can judge people properly. He himself is very laborious bearing the pains of the sun, rain, cold, crossing over rivers, takes up wrestling and riding. He does not know what is fear. He is expert in impersonations. He is also skilled in investigating matters in disguise. His tongue is so sweet that whoever meets him once, always praises him. He always inquires of people if they have met any hermit or any skilled person. If yes, he keeps on talking about them in detail for long: If the person was the famous Baba Tukaram of Dehu? Did he preach his sermons here? Did he sing '*Bhajans*'? He even forgets his hunger and thirst while asking these questions. Wherever he goes, people gather around him. He talks of battles and bravery. What to talk of his wanderings? If he is here today, tomorrow you will find him 50 miles away from here. Nobody walks arrogantly before him. If so, he nabs him. He imitates the voices of birds and animals so nicely that nobody can differentiate. He does not know any hurdle. He has introspective eyes. All the 'Deshmukhs', big or small, of the Mawal only praise him."

Dadaji Konddeo was popular. His dutifulness, patriotism and selflessness were uncomparable. He left no stone unturned to make Shivaji as he and Jijabai had thought of. He started touring villages after he took charge of the estate. He took along Shivaji also on these tours. In order to bring peace and prosperity to the estate he started organising panchayats, settling disputes, and constructing ponds and tanks for agricultural purposes. He seated Shivaji, dressed in royal robes, at the main seat in the panchayat and told the people, "Now, he is the master of you all. You should obey him. If you walk beyond the track, he will control you. If you are on the right path, he will bring welfare to you."

Dadaji's such efforts brought awareness in the whole state. People, who had been being tortured for centuries, also started dreaming of an independent Hindu state. They started looking at Shivaji as their real king and the centre of their hopes. Wherever Shivaji visited, people touched his feet and listened to his words with great respect.

The condition of the state started improving within two to three years. People managed the guards of their villages. They also managed the protection of their fields from the wild animals. As a result the agricultural products increased significantly. He produced the account of all the incomes and expenditures of the estate before Shivaji and took further steps on his instruction. This brought a good improvement in the economic condition of Jijabai and Shivaji. The fate of Jijabai started taking turns who had been completely abandoned by her husband. She herself began to attend panchayats and started giving decisions also.

The credit for all these improvements must go to Dadaji Konddeo who did all this with such selflessness and true determination which is a unique example in the history. Certainly, his contribution is an example in its own. He never forgot his prime duty for even a moment. And the utmost fact is that he was custodian of not only Shivaji but Jijabai also.

Education and Training of Shivaji

When the estate came under full control, Jijabai started worrying about Shivaji's education. A priest (*Pandit*) was arranged to teach him religion and politics. He was also given the knowledge of the *Ramayana* and the *Mahabharata*. He was educated in alphabets and elementary mathematics by Pantoji. Shivaji became very trustful to his mother due to the religious education given to him.

They say that Shivaji was illiterate, but it is not true. Though he didn't receive regular education, he was not completely illiterate. Though there is no clear evidence of this, but the historians are against the thought of Shivaji being illiterate. It is right that his education could not start at proper age. He was about 10-15 years of age when he was taught the alphabet. Without getting proper education he performed such works which we can't even hope from well-educated people.

Marriage

Mother Jijabai played the role of the father in Shivaji's life. Shahji was busy in conquering Karnataka for Bijapur from 1638 to 1640. Jijabai's elder son Sambhaji and Shahji's second wife's son Ekoji were with Shahji. On the other hand Shivaji was developing under the affection of mother Jijabai and the custodianship of Dadaji Konddeo. She arranged Shivaji's marriage with Saibai, a girl from the Nimbalkar family of Falton, in 1640. Evidently, neither the father nor the brothers could attend his marriage.

It is worth mentioning here that it was Shivaji's first marriage. Historians say that he had made seven more marriages and it was not wrong according to the tradition then. Sumanbai, Soyarabai, Putlabai, Laxmibai, Sakwarbai, Kashibai and Gunwantibai were the names of Shivaji's seven wives other than Saibai.

Shivaji's first marriage took place when he was 12-13 years of age. The modern society will call it a child-marriage but it was a normal feature those days. Probably Jijabai's motherly affection was the reason behind it.

Father-Son Meeting

The estate of Shahji Bhonsle was prospering under the supervision of Dadaji Konddeo. He got all this report regularly and naturally he was very happy but a few administrative officers of Bijapur were not happy at Shivaji's progress. They got the news that Shivaji, under the custodianship of Dadaji Konddeo and mother Jijabai, was ignoring the administrative officers of Bijapur posted there. Shivaji had managed his estate well and had organised his people well. He had also got the old forts repaired and collected all necessary things there. Naturally Bijapur was alarmed at this.

Shahji could not have met his wife and son for last four years. He was getting all the above doubtful news. Moreover, he was also very eager to see his newly married daughter-in-law. Hence, he summoned all of them to Bangalore. Jijabai, Dadaji Konddeo, Shivaji and Saibai went to see him at Bangalore in 1640.

Shahji was a loyal officer of the Muslim kingdom. He had destroyed all the Hindu states situated around the kingdom. On the contrary Dadaji Konddeo, Jijabai and Shivaji all were full of the ideology of the Hindu culture and had been dreaming of an independent Hindu state.

In the Court of Bijapur

Jijabai and Shivaji were planning to return when suddenly Shahji was summoned to the court. He, therefore, took his son along to the court of Bijapur. It was the custom of the court that the visitor had to bow down touching the ground with his head in order to pay respect to the crown. Shahji did the same which Shivaji felt as a heinous act. He also saluted the king in the Maratha style which contained all the respect in itself, but it was not at all a '*Sijdah*'. The king took it to be rudeness and disrespect to him. He asked for an explanation from Shahji for this. Shahji replied that Shivaji was an illiterate village boy who did not know the customs of the court and requested to pardon his offence, whereas he knew it very well that Shivaji hated Muslims for their tyranny.

There was a big difference between the thinkings of the father and the son. Hence, Jijabai and Shivaji decided to go back. It is essential to mention here that Jijabai got no pleasure on meeting Shahji, her husband. Clearly, the reasons were Shahji's devotion to the Muslims and his behaviour towards his wife. On the one hand he had almost abandoned Jijabai and on the other hand he was bringing up his new family well. After all, Jijabai was also a woman. Probably she would have felt that Shahji had called her there to tease her. She, therefore, left Shivaji with Dadaji Konddeo and set out for a one-year pilgrimage to Kanchi Rameshwar. Dadaji Konddeo managed so that their relation did not divert more.

It is said that during his visit to Bijapur he saw a butcher taking a cow for slaughter. Shivaji immediately drew out his sword and chopped off his head. This incident was probed into. So, in order to avoid any future problem, he had to leave Bijapur.

Jijabai had returned to Bangalore from the pilgrimage. She was also not in favour of staying in Bangalore anymore. Hence, both Jijabai and Shivaji along with all their servants left for Poona either by the end of 1642 or in the beginning of 1643. Dadaji Konddeo had already gone to Poona. Shahji had arranged accoutrements for an independent estate's court before Shivaji left. Apart from this, he also gave him infantry, horse riders, war elephants, valuable flags, estate symbol and a lot of wealth. They say that Shahji had sent Shyaurao Neelkanth (Peshwa), Bal Krishna Pant (Majurdar), Balaji Hariji (Courtier), Raghunath Ballal (Korde), Sono Pant (Daber) and Raghunath Atre (Chitnish) for better and efficient running of Shivaji's estate. This clarifies that Shahji also wanted to see his son, Shivaji, as an independent ruler, but circumstances did not allow him to support Shivaji openly. Had he done so, probably Shivaji won't be able to attain his goal. This shows the practical farsightedness of Shahji.

After returning to Poona, Shivaji started his efforts for the establishment of an independent Hindu state. He was sure that his father also was a supporter of his ideology. Shivaji was now heading towards his youthdom. At this state he had many childhood mates who were his true friends who could even sacrifice their lives for Shivaji.

Two

Administration

The Then Social and Political Situation

The era of Hindu humiliation started as soon as the Muslim rule set foot in India. It rose to the optimum during the reign of Aurangjeb. Maharashtra was also not spared. The Hindu temples were demolished, idols were smashed to pieces and every now and then you could hear of some atrocity or the other. These Muslim atrocities have been very clearly mentioned in the religious literature of the Deccan. Hermits kept on roaming throughout the country. They noticed the same worst condition of the people everywhere. They prayed to God, "O Lord! You incarnated to destroy the atrocities of Ravana etc. time to time and salvaged the earth. Now also there is the same situation. Then, why are you keeping your eyes closed? Don't you take pity on our pitiable condition? Please save us!"

The Hindus were forcibly converted to Islam. Almost all the Hindu rulers had surrendered to the Muslims. Almost all the dynasties of the Deccan had become a subject of history. Shivaji had felt all this in his early age. He faced it after taking the charge of the state of Poona. This state had also gone under the Muslim rule. His mother, Jijabai, had been frequently telling him the stories of bravery of the Indians since his childhood. She also told him how Nizamshah and brutally slaughtered her father and brothers and how Bajaji Nimbalkar, a kin of Shahji's maternal grandfather, had been forcibly converted into a Muslim. Similar incidencts had been occurring throughout the country. Dadaji Konddeo also told Shivaji all about it.

Shivaji, a lad, gradually understood all his duties and responsibilities. His thoughts started gaining maturity with the growing age. His mother, Jijabai, and Dadaji Konddeo were hopeful when they observed Shivaji's works and style. They were now assured that their efforts were not going in vain. They praised Shivaji's works. This raised Shivaji's spirits. The child Shivaji started progressing under the custodianship of these two guardians and also his popularity in the state kept growing. However, mother Jijabai and Dadaji Konddeo were not satisfied with Shivaji's fame and popularity. They wanted to see him as an independent Hindu ruler.

Beginning of the Dream Fulfilment

Shivaji started laying the foundation stone of his mission after he returned to Poona getting the silent approval of his father. He constituted an organisation of his childhood mates who were still underaged (not adult). Members of this organisation were always ready to help him and if required they could even sacrifice their lives. Shivaji became determined to establish an independent state. He started discussing the matter with his faithful friends. Gomaji Nayak Pansambal, Yesaji Kuk, Tanaji Malsure, Baji Pasalkar and Bajirao Jedhe were some prominent friends of Shivaji, though the number of these friends had reached the four-figure mark. Shivaji always got the advices and guidence from his best well-wishing custodian, Dadaji Konddeo, in these matters.

Shivaji and his friends started surveying big and small forts, secret paths, wharfs etc of the Mawal province riding on horses. Spies were appointed who gathered information about the local Muslim officers and their whereabouts, what arrangements they had made in their forts, how did the guards of the forts work, evils in them, their weaknesses and what arrangements were to be made to attack these forts. They also started observing the internal situation of the Mawal province joining the caravans, and going into the temples, markets and fairs.

Shivaji used to speak against the Muslim tyranny in order to raise the spirits of his people. He said, "The foreigner Muslims are outraging our country and our religion. Is it not our duty to fight against this? It is very essential. Why should we be satisfied with only our paternal property and awards from the Muslim? We are Hindu, this whole country is ours but the Muslims are the rulers here. They are desecrating our holy temples, destroying the idols, robbing our wealth, converting our people forcibly into Muslims and slaughtering of *Go Mata*. Now, we will not tolerate all this. We have strength. We have to draw our swords to protect our religion. We will get our motherland freed from them. We will occupy new estate and wealth with our own efforts. We are brave and self-sufficient like our forefathers. Once we start this holy mission, God will automatically help us. A man must get success if he tries within the sources available. There is nothing like fortune or misfortune."

His words raised the spirits of his enthusiastic friends and their arms started throbbing to get the motherland free. Shivaji captured twelve passes of Mawal, very soon captured the fort of Kaurhana and renamed it 'Singhgarh'. As soon as this news reached Bijapur, Shahji was removed from the court and the Sultan sent a message to Kanhoji Jedhe on 16th August, 1644 which read:

"Shahji Bhonsle has been insulted and removed from the court. We have got the news that his representative Dadaji Konddeo has started rebellious activities in the Kaurhana Fort. Khandoji and Baji Ghorpade have been assigned the job of suppressing him and of proving our hold on the province. Hence, you are ordered through this letter to assist Ghorpade along with your whole army and to destroy the cunning rebel Dadaji Konddeo and his followers with full force. You will be properly rewarded on the successful execution of this order."

Kanhoji Jedhe was a very good friend of Shahji and a strong supporter of Shivaji. Probably he didn't took any action in this matter so he was also imprisoned along with Shahji Bhonsle.

Resolution of a Free Hindu Self Government

Shivaji was much encouraged by his above success. Hence, he pledged for a free Hindu self-government on 30th of March, 1645. After taking this vow he isued his official coin on which the following ideal sentences were engraved. "This coin of Shivaji, the son of Shahji Bhonsle, is only for the welfare of the people. It grows regularly like the new moon and the world is to pay respect to it." He created new posts and appointed people on them for proper functioning of the government. And then he started working hard for the attainment of his goal. First of all he decided to capture the neighbouring forts and captured the Torana, Chakan and other forts within a short time.

Capture of the Torana Fort

Shivaji captured the Torana Fort without much effort in 1646. They say that he had given a huge amount to the security guard of the fort as bribe and brought him in his favour. He had got huge wealth hidden underground in this fort. After this he began to pretend to others that he had done good to the Sultan by doing this. He sent his representative to the Sultan to convince him that it was very wise to have a strong security force protecting such a lonely fort. The representatives also told the Sultan that Shivaji did all this only due to his faithfulness to Bijapur. The court accepted their straddle. Shivaji gave away the land around the fort to the Deshmukhs so that they should not oppose him. At the same time he gave away bulky amounts to many of the courtiers of Bijapur in bribe and thus diverted the attention of Bijapur from himself and his works. There his representatives kept the court of Bijapur busy in discussions through these arguments and Shivaji on the other hand was busy in including the Mawal people in his army. He also started the repair work of the Torana Fort to increase his strength. He found the above mentioned wealth during this repair work only. This huge wealth solved most of Shivaji's problems. He purchased a good quantity of arms for his army and also started the construction of a new fort. This fort was built on the Morebudh hill which was three miles to the south-east from the Torana Fort.

The information about the construction of a new fort also reached Bijapur. Bijapur issued an order to stop the construction and a letter of objection was sent to Shahji in which he was asked to clarify the justification of this work. Shahji wrote the reply to Bijapur which read, "Though Shivaji did not take my consent in the construction of this fort still since my whole family is in the service of Bijapur, Shivaji must be building this fort for the security of the state and also for the prosperity of the kingdom."

Shahji wrote a letter to Dadaji Konddeo asking the reason of the construction and also ordered to stop the work. Dadaji gave all the information to Shivaji and advised him to stop the work for the sake of Shahji's security reason. Shivaji listened to all what Dadaji told him very politely but did not stop the construction work.

Dadaji Konddeo passed away on 7th March, 1647 only a few days after the Torana Fort was captured. He called Shivaji before dying and said, "Raje!. Now everything is on your shoulder. I did and told you the things that I found right till date. You keep on trying honestly and the Almighty will bestow fame on you. The plant of self-government has been sown. Just keep on protecting it."

The death of Dadaji Konddeo was such a personal loss to Shivaji and his mother Jijabai that could not be made up. Hence, it is most obvious that they would have been shocked to a large extent at his death, but this could not deter Shivaji. He always remembered the dying words of Dadaji Konddeo. These words inspired him a lot. Now he was planning to give an open challenge to Bijapur. He required a lot of wealth for this. Hence, he took full charge of the estate's management and started considering upon the income and expenditure very wisely. Dadaji Konddeo always sent the details of income and expenditure of the estate to Shahji. Shahji took a part of the land revenue. After the death of Dadaji, one of Shahji's messangers came to take Shahji's share. Shivaji told him that the estate was unable to spare money as the expenditure of the estate has gone up due to the death of Dadaji. That day onward he always sent back the messanger without paying even a single farthing. And in the end he sent the message to Shahji that Poona was unable to spare money as the expenses on the subject and also an administration had grown up very steeply. Shahji might maintain his expenses from his well-to-do estate of Karnataka.

Capturing Chakan

The officers of Chakan and Supe were opposed to Shivaji. It was necessary for him either to turn these officers in his favour or to remove them from there if he had to occupy these forts. Firangiji Narsal was the guard at the Chakan Fort. Shivaji very soon got him to favour him. Thus he could easily capture the Chakan Fort in 1648. This was an open challenge to the Bijapur kingdom. After capturing the fort he made

Firangiji the chieftain of the Chakan Fort and also assigned him the right of managing the revenue collection in the neighbouring villages.

Capturing Purandar

The Purandar Fort was situated to the south-east of Poona. The custodian of this fort was Neelkanth Sarnayak who was involved in disputes with his brothers. Shivaji requested Sarnayak to allow him shelter in the fort for a few days during the rains in 1648. He got the permission. Shivaji set up his camp just below the fort. The brothers of Sarnayak requested Shivaji to settle their dispute. It seems as if they also requested him to imprison Sarnayak and occupy the fort. Suddenly Sarnayak invited Shivaji and his mother into the fort on the occasion of Diwali. Shivaji was ready for this. He ordered his soldiers to surround the fort from all around in the night. When he went into the fort in the night, the custodian Sarnayak and his brothers were captured while they were sleeping and the fort was conquered. All these brothers after a long discussion among themselves accepted the subjugation to Shivaji and promised to remain loyal to him. Then they were set free. Thus Shivaji captured the Purandar Fort without any bloodshed only by his political cleverness. Neelkanth Sarnayak and his brothers remained in the service of the Maratha dynasty for ever.

Bijapur's Anger for Shahji

Shrirang Roy was crowned to the almost worn out throne of Vijay Nagar in 1642. He immediately started to check the situation and captured Vellore. At this Bijapur kingdom sent a huge army against him. Shrirang Roy was badly defeated in 1646. The Sultan of Bijapur got the information that Shahji was secretly helping Shrirang Roy. Almost at the same time Shivaji had started revolt by capturing Kaurhana. And the capture of Chakan by Shivaji was an open challenge to the Sultan of Bijapur. The Bijapur state formed their opinion that Shahji was behind all this mischief. Hence, Shahji was arrested on 25th of July 1648 very dramatically. Immediately after this, an army was sent from Bijapur to invade Singhgarh. There was a fierce battle and the Bijapur army was defeated. This success of Shivaji gave the Bijapur kingdom a good knowledge of his strength.

Sambhaji, the elder son of Shahji, had also captured Bangalore. Hence, the captive Shahji was brought to Bijapur. Adilshah, the Sultan of Bijapur, could not give any cruel treatment to Shahji, who was the father of two brave sons Sambhaji and Shivaji. Also, he was suffering from paralysis that time, so it was better for him to compromise with Shahji. Shahji also clarified that neither he himself nor his sons were opposed to the Sultan. Only he needed sufficient area for doing respectful work and support in the court of Bijapur. He was ready to work with loyalty to Bijapur if he would get those things. The Sultan accepted his proposal. Then Shahji wrote letters to Shivaji and Sambhaji to surrender the forts of Bangalore and Singhgarh to Bijapur for the sake of Shahji's life.

Release of Shahji

Shivaji got the news of Shahji's arrest almost immediately. That time Shahjada Muradbaksh was the governor of the Deccan. Shivaji thought to take the help of Muradbaksh for the release of his father. There was a good deal of correspondence between them. In the meantime Muradbaksh went to Delhi assuring Shivaji that he wold talk to emperor Shahjehan in this matter. Probably, there was no progress in this matter.

Sambhaji and Shivaji got the letters sent by their father. Shivaji talked to his mother on this topic. Jijabai, for the sake of her husbands' life, directed her sons to surrender the forts to the Sultan of Bijapur. The sons probably were not unanimous. So, Sambhaji requested Shivaji to get the advice of his advisor Sonopant. Sonopant was a skilled politician. He told Shivaji that all the doors of the world are always open for brave people, hence, he should accept the advice of Jijabai in order to save the life of his father. Later the two forts could be recaptured. So, after surrendering these two forts to Bijapur, Shahji was released on 16th May, 1649 after an imprisonment of almost ten months.

The above description is given by Sardesai. Grand Dough has described the imprisonment of Shahji in some other way. According to him, Awaji Sondeo, after conquering Kalyan, arrested Mulla Ahmad, Bijapur's representative there and brought him to Poona, but Shivaji set him free. The Sultan of Bijapur thought that Shahji was behind all these. By this time Shahji had achieved quite a good status. He was enjoying the post of the governor in his province. So the Sultan thought it better to put an end to his powers. On the insistence of the Sultan, Baji Ghorpade invited Shahji to dinner and arrested him there. He was then allowed to make correspondence with Shivaji. Shahji told the Sultan that he was loyal to Bijapur and opposed to Shivaji like the Sultan but the Sultan did not believed it. He was imprisoned in a dark dungeon and even the door was also brick-laid. Only there was a small hole. He was threatened that if Shivaji did not surrender within the given time period, that hole would also be blocked.

Shivaji decided to surrender when he got this information. But his wife, Saibai, stopped him from taking such a suicidal action. Then he approached the Mughal emperor, Shahjahan, for his father's release through Morar Pant. Earlier Shahji had worked under the emperor but later had left him. After a long discussion the emperor forgave Shahji for his old offences and agreed to take his services and also provided him with an army of five hundred horses. Thus he was freed from the prison of Bijapur though he had to remain in the prison for four long years.

Capture of Supa

There was another fort of Supa near Poona. Sambhaji Mohite, a representative of Bijapur, was the custodian of this fort. The special feature was that Sambhaji was the brother of Tukabai, Shivaji's stepmother, but he was jealous of Shivaji's progress. Moreover, he was a loyal servant of Bijapur. It was very essential for Shivaji to conquer this fort, so he requested his maternal uncle to help capture him the fort, but he did not agree to it at any cost. Shivaji had a top class trained army comprising of 300 brave soldiers. One dark night Shivaji invaded the fort of Supa with all these soldiers. Sambhaji Mohite got no time to get ready, so he was arrested and his entire wealth was looted. He was again asked to join hands with Shivaji,.but he did not agree. So he was sent to Shahji in Bangalore with a special security force as a captive. The details of the action taken against Sambhaji was also sent to Shahji. Thus Supa also came under the possession of Shivaji very easily. Probably it had happened between 1649 and 1652.

Shivaji did not require to shed even a single drop of blood to capture these forts. Now he was busy in maintaining good management in his territories.

Declaration of an Independent State

Thus Shivaji occupied the region from Chakan to the river Neera. He made proper security arrangement in the forts of Chakan, Purandar, Supa and Baramati to strengthen his status. Till now he was only working in the hilly areas. He had a special thought in his mind behind not invading the plain areas. He wanted to increase his strength first. He therefore started to manage the territories he had already conquered. He knew it well that an estate can flourish only with the support of the people. He, therefore, tried for long seven years to win the goodwill of his subjects. During this period he visited different parts of his estate. There were trade centres of the British, the Dutch and the Europeans in the coastal cities. He made friends with all of them. His motive behind this was only that he could get their help while expanding his estate in future.

Shivaji's above efforts made his people happy and prosperous. Now he was sure that he had full hold over this region. In the beginning he ruled over this estate as the representative of Shahji, but after Shahji was freed from Bijapur he found it useless to do so. Within a span of ten years of his first win—conquering the fort of Kaurhana (Singhgarh)—he felt as if he should declare his estate as an independent one. Hence, he declared his full independence in 1653.

In fact a lion is never coronated or crowned, he is called the '*Vanraja*' only due to its might. The same definition is fit for Shivaji also. When he was born his mother was leading the life of a destitute. It is beyond description the hardships and difficulties in his upbringing and protection. Shivaji became an independent ruler only in the twenty-fifth year of his age.

Three

Sequence of Successes

Now, Shivaji had become a fully independent ruler. He had increased his strength so much that he was self-sufficient to protect his kingdom. The historian Dough writes about his strength: "He had gripped the whole region with the vigilance of a leopard. He continued to gather his strength in the hills only till he was sure that he was fully secured. When people started to assess his strength by his rise, they were able to understand that Shivaji had become so strong that he could face any type of problem. So, then, he decided to expand his state using his strength."

All the chieftains of Mawal accepted his leadership seeing his strength. But still there were a few who considered themselves of high families and Shivaji of a lower caste. There was the state of Jawali at the foot of the Mahabaleshwar hill. It was under More family. The More were considered to be the descendants of Chandragupta Maurya whereas the Bhosle were taken to be the '*shudras*'. More were an ancient 'Deshmukh' family and were respected in the society. Shivaji tried a lot to bring them in his favour, but in vain. It was not possible for Shivaji to tolerate such an enemy in the neighbourhood. He thought a lot on how to throw this thorn away. He wanted to sideline him getting the lowest loss.

Earlier he had tried many a time to make friends with them. When Shivaji declared his independence and held the title of 'Chhatrapati', it became intolerable to the More family. Jawali was situated at such a place that it was fully secured. Their family pride provoked them to oppose Shivaji openly. They began to ignore Shivaji at the support of Bijapur. To end up this bitterness Shivaji proposed to establish marriage relations with the More family, but they didn't agree to it due to their family pride. They clearly denied any type of ties with him. At this Shivaji threatened them of revenge. In reply to his threat, they insulted him saying, "The reply to your threat is that we accept this proposal. Instead of coming in future, come now and bring an army as large as you wish. You claim to be an independent king. Who accepts you a king? A young boy of yesterday claims to be a king today. You can boast as much as you wish at home, who cares? Come to Jawali and see how you are welcomed. We respect the honour that the Sultan of Bijapur has given us. It is our prime duty to obey his orders, whatever may happen."

Thus the More family left no stone unturned in insulting Shivaji. Apart from this, they wore the title of Kutawatans to declare that they were superior Kshatriya so that they could look down upon Shivaji.

Probably the end of the More family was approaching which is therefore that they gave a practical shape to the proverb, "Vainglorious though vanquished" due to their false family pride; otherwise they could have also saved themselves like other Deshmukh families.

Afzal Khan was appointed governor of Bai by Bijapur in 1649. This intensified the odd situation of Shivaji. In fact Afzal Khan was sent only to suppress Shivaji, hence he started encouraging the More people to oppose Shivaji. This time a man named Hanumant Rao More was the ruler of Jawali as Daulatrao More had died in 1648 without leaving any heir. His widow had adopted a son and was running the administration with the help of Hanumant Rao More, one of her relatives. The More people had become stronger with the presence of Afzal Khan, but suddenly he was transferred from Bai to Kanakgiri. Shivaji took it as an opportunity for him. Hence Shivaji drew Kanhoji Jedhe, Haiwat Rao Silibhkar and some of the near relatives of the More family in his favour in 1655. Shivaji again sent the proposal of collaboration to the More family through these people and also sent a small army under the leadership of his commander Sambhaji Kaoji. The army surrounded his house and the Deshmukhs went to the More family with the proposal which the More did not accept. The army charged, but could not succeed. Hence another army under Raghunath Ballal Korde was sent. Both the armies met near Jawali and faught a battle in which Hanumant Rao More was killed. Yashwant Rao fled away and reached the Raduri Fort. One other member of the family fled to Bijapur and started planning to oust Shivaji from Jawali with the help of Adil Shah. Shivaji himself reached Jawali in January 1656 and captured Jawali on the 26th of January 1656. He stayed there for further two months. Yashwant Rao again started preparing against Shivaji from Raduri, so Shivaji had to send an army there also. He also sent his messenger Haiwat Rao Silibhkar with a proposal to Yashwant Rao to surrender. After a long debate the More people became ready to talk to Shivaji. It was decided that they would meet beneath the Raduri Fort but as soon as Yashwant Rao reached there, Shivaji got him killed and his two sons, Krishnaji More and Baji More, arrested. They were taken to Poona after the arrest. Later they were also caught conspiring against Shivaji and were killed.

Shivaji had never done such a cruel action in his whole life. He always showed kindness and respect to those who were arrested. Such deceit did not match a great warrior like Shivaji. The historians have quoted it as a black spot on his clean character. Such a cruel deed due to personal enmity is not good.

After capturing Jawali Shivaji became the lone ruler of the twelve Mawals from Junnar to Bai. After this he planned to establish his control over the valley of Parghat. For this he started constructing a new fort at Pratapgarh under the supervision of his most faithful servant Moropant Pingle. Before this Moropant Pingle was in the service of his father in Karnataka. An idol of Bhagawati Bhawani was installed in the fort. Mata Jijabai often came to this fort to live. Shivaji was much pleased with Moropant Pingle due to the construction of this fort. Hence, he was made the new Peshwa after Peshwa Shyamraj Pant died in 1662.

Loot of Junnar and Ahmednagar

Till then Shivaji had neither attacked nor captured any Mughal territory. In 1657 he felt that he could do this. It is better to give a short description of the then Mughal empire first. Aurangzeb was born on October 1618 and thus he was older than Shivaji by nine years. He had been going to the battlefield with his father when he was a youth. He also took part in the battle in which Shahjehan defeated Nizamshah. Shahjehan returned to north after the battle. Aurangzeb became the governor of south in 1636. He was assigned the work to manage the territories won by the Mughals. He retained this post till 1644. After this he was busy in the battles in the north-west. He again became the governor of the south from 1653 to 1658. Shivaji did not do anything special during Aurangzeb's first tenure, so the Mughal empire had no fear from him.

A lot of changes had taken place in the south by the time Aurangzeb came for the second time as the governor of south. During this period Shivaji had been making his empire stronger without disturbing the Mughals. When Shivaji increased his activities in 1657, it was natural that Aurangzeb noted it. Shivaji found it necessary to warn the Mughal empire. Hence, after capturing Jawali in 1657 he attacked the Mughal territories of Junnar and Ahmednagar and looted them.

Capturing Konkan

That time the commodities for internal trade were brought to the coasts of Kalyan and Basai and were taken away by that route only. These were the main centres of trade and the fertile coastal plains were controlled from here only. Shivaji had more benefit if he captured these, at the same time it could be well protected as Poona was very near to it. Shivaji's spies were on regular patrol of this area. Shivaji himself went there for observation. That territory was under the control of Bijapur and Mulla Ahmad was the governor there. In 1655 Shivaji's spies informed him that the Sultan of Bijapur had instructed Mulla Ahmad to carry all the revenue collected from Kalyan to Bijapur. Shivaji planned to rob this treasure. For this a troop was instructed to rob the treasure when it would be passing the Purandar road. Another troop was sent to attack Kalyan. When the treasure was being robbed near Poona, Peshawa Shyauraj Neelkanth and his cousin Dadaji Bapuji attacked Kalyan. The governor was with the treasure. The plan was successful. The treasure was brought to the Rajgarh fort and Kalyan was also captured. In the meantime Bhiwandi was also captured.

Security arrangements were made on the Port of Kalyan after this victory. The forts in Mahuli and the north-south of Kalyan were also captured. Chaul, Tale, Ghosle, Ramchi, Lohgarh, Kangori, Turangtikon etc. were also soon captured.

By October 1657, the whole of Konkan had been captured. Abaji Sonedeo was made the governor of Kalyan.

An interesting incident during the Konkan victory is famous. When Abaji Sonedeo was made the governor of Kalyan, by chance he got the most beautiful daughter-in-law of the ex-governor. He thought that she should be sent to Shivaji as a gift. Probably, the young Shivaji will be happy getting such a gift. So, she was sent to Poona for Shivaji with full security. Shivaji showed full respect to the lady and said, "Ah! I wish my mother were also beautiful like you!" Begging pardon from her he sent her home with full respect. He warned Sonedeo and all his associates not to do this in future and to any other lady they should show respect as they do to their mother.

After winning Konkan Shivaji had control over a triangular region from Basai to Rajapur near the sea coast. He could not capture Prabalgarh near Panwal. This fort was under the supervision of sepoy Keshari Singh under the Bijapur empire. Shivaji along with his army went to capture the fort. Keshari Singh was killed in the battle. Shivaji got a treasure full of gold bars and gold coins buried in the fort. Keshari Singh's mother and his two children hid due to fright who were later caught by the soldiers. Shivaji saluted the mother of Keshari Singh and sent her to her birthplace, Dewalgaon, in a palanquin escorted by security guards. The funeral of the soldiers who were killed protecting the fort was done with full respect.

After this Shivaji looted Junnar and his army reached Ahmadnagar. Ahmadnagar was saved by the strong security force but the army of Shivaji looted the other parts of the state with full force. At that time Junnar was under Mughal empire so the Mughal governor of south, Aurangzeb, was taken aback. Shivaji did not want any clash with him so he sent Krishnaji Bhaskar as his messenger to convince Aurangzeb about the justification of his deeds and also to tell him that the forts of the northern Konkan which were under Bijapur were now under Shivaji.

In the meantime Aurangzeb had to return to Delhi when Shahjahan fell ill so that his brothers did not ascend the throne, but before leaving he ordered his men to keep strict control over Shivaji's activities.

Now, Shivaji started making arrangements for public

welfare in his territories, so people began to live in peace and happiness. After north Konkan, Shivaji went to south and started examining the security arrangements. After completing his tour he came back to Rajgarh and discussed with his men about the administrative works in the state. He very strictly suppressed arbitrary exploitation. He selected experienced people from among the Deshpandeys and Deshmukhs and appointed them on respectable posts. He captured many more forts either by cheating or forcibly and appointed faithful people to protect them. He awarded those who worked with labour and honesty and those who did not were expelled.

On increase in the administrative works more new people were appointed. Nilo Somedeo, the brother of Abaji Somedeo, was made *Majumdar*, Gangu Mangaji was made *Wakenaweesh* and Anaji Datto the secretary. Netaji Palkar was made the commander at the death of Sarnaubwat Mankoji Risale. The most competent and faithful Abaji was appointed at the post of Chitnis.

The Bhawani *Kripan* (dagger)

Shivaji had named his *Kripan* 'Bhawani'. This *Kripan* was very dear to him. Actually he had bought it from Kudal. Shivaji spent the whole year of 1657 in touring his provinces and managing administration. Rustame Zama attacked Kudal in the summers of 1658. The ruler there was also of the Bhonsle family. He requested for Shivaji's help against this attack. So Shivaji went towards Rajapur via Hareshwar temple in order to help him. He saved Kudal from Rustame Zama in the battle. Hence, next year, in 1659, there was a pact between the two to help each other. He bought a European *Kripan* for three hundred hones from the market of Kudal when he had gone there to sign the pact and named it 'Bhawani'.

Formation of Naval Fleet

Shivaji was a multitalented person. He felt the need of a strong naval force after the establishment of his state. For this he, first of all, made a sailors' fort named Vijay Fort, the construction work of which had started in 1653. Another sailors' fort, the Swarn Fort, was built in 1660 then again in 1664 the third one, Sindhu Fort, was built. He made a very big naval base, Kulaba, in 1680.

Afzal Khan Episode

After the death of Sultan Mohammad Adil Shah on 4th November, 1656, Bijapur was surrounded by misfortunes from all sides. On the one hand there was Mughal attacks and on the other hand Shivaji was expanding his empire. The eldest wife (*Begum*) of the departed Sultan was ruling in the name of her minor son but she had no hold or influence on the people. Even those Muslim *sardars*, who were once considered faithful, had become rebels. In fact Bijapur state had been almost shattered. Shivaji had captured the province of Maratha and in Karnataka his father's rule had been established.

Whatever the condition of the state was, it was necessary to save it from Shivaji. In this context, Shahji was requested to stop Shivaji from attacking Bijapur. At this Shahji told that he was not responsible for any activity of Shivaji. Whatever action the Bijapur government wishes, it can take against Shivaji.

Shivaji had increased his attacks on Bijapur after Aurangzeb had left South India. It was a question of life or death for Bijapur to suppress Shivaji but none of the *samants* dared to do so. Finally, this assignment went to Afzal Khan who was the illegal son of the Sultan of Bijapur. His mother worked as a cook in the royal kitchen. He had taken part in many battles in Karnataka so he had a good name. He was jealous of Shahji and his sons from the beginning, so he found a good opportunity to take revenge. The *begum* advised him to arrest Shivaji alive or dead. In fact Afzal Khan did not require any such advice. He left for his destination in September, 1656. Shivaji was perhaps in the Pratapgarh Fort. Earlier, Afzal Khan had worked as the governor of Bai so he was well acquainted with this region. He had twelve thousand soldiers with him. He reached Rahimatpur via Pandharpur, Mahadevi mountain range and Malwadi. He desecrated all the temples he found on his way and broke all the idols. He demolished the famous temples of Tuljapur, a famous pilgrimage in Maharashtra. He broke the idol of Tulja Bhawani in Tuljapur. Bajaji Nimbalkar was a special victim of his anger because he was first converted to Muslim forcibly by the ruler of Bijapur but later Shivaji again converted him into a Hindu.

Shivaji had a very close eye on all his activities from Rajgarh. He had decided to encounter him near Bai and Jawali. He fixed his stay in the Pratapgarh Fort. Mata Jijabai was also here. Khan had the information that Shivaji was in Pratapgarh Fort so he camped about 16 miles away from Pratapgarh. There was the high plateau of Mahabaleshwar between Pratapgarh and his army camp. Both the enemies were face to face so both of them now started thinking about the battle. The Pratapgarh Fort was on a high and unaccessible hilltop where open battle was not possible and Afzal Khan could not take his huge army there in any way so Shivaji was well-protected in the fort. He was in search of a chance when he could capture his enemy, Afzal Khan, easily. On the other hand Afzal Khan was thinking how he could draw his enemy out of the fort so that he could kill the snake without a stake. Undoubtedly both of them were in a tense situation.

Finally, Khan lost his patience and decided to call Shivaji out of the fort for compromise. For this he required a very faithful person, so he chose Krishnaji Bhaskar of Bai who was a very loyal servant of Bijapur. He was sent to Shivaji with the message that Afzal Khan had friendly feelings for Shivaji and his family. If he willingly accepts Bijapur's mastery, he would be welcomed and given a respectable post like his father in the Bijapur state. It was also possible to reach a compromise with Bijapur on his terms. Thus Khan wanted to arrest Shivaji without any bloodshed taking him into confidence.

Krishnaji came to Shivaji with Khan's message. He executed his work very cleverly and honestly, but Shivaji had a very sharp brain. He was well aware of Khan's history. He could very easily understand the meaning of this assurance but he concealed his feelings. He expressed his faithfulness to Bijapur and father-like respect for Afzal Khan and said that he had done a very idiotic work and requested Afzal Khan to pull him out of this crisis. In fact Shivaji wanted to extend this debate longer.

Krishnaji Bhaskar was given a splendid place to stay. Shivaji alone approached Krishnaji in the lonely dwelling and appealed to him to favour Hinduism and Brahmanism and requested him to help in the establishment of a Hindu state.

Probably a huge amount was given to him as a bribe in the form of gift. Here, the historians give different opinions. Some say that he told Shivaji about Khan's true intention, some others say that he remained faithful to his master, but it is for sure that he was influenced by Shivaji.

After this Shivaji sent his own messenger, Pantaji Gopinath along with Krishnaji Bhaskar to Afzal Khan. He gave Afzal Khan Shivaji's message that he did not want to fight such big army. He repented on whatever he did against Bijapur. If Afzal Khan forgave him and exempted his life, he would return all the provinces he had won from Bijapur.

Shivaji's messenger, Pantaji Gopinath, was very faithful and a clever politician. He requested Khan that if he really wanted to forgive Shivaji, he could fearlessly meet him in the Pratapgarh Fort itself. Nobody could carry his army over to that place so there was no risk in meeting him there. Pantaji Gopinath very cleverly persuaded him to meet Shivaji at the foot of the Pratapgarh Fort and he also assured Khan that once they had a meeting, Shivaji would do only what Khan ordered. At this Khan had the confidence that he could achieve his goal without fighting a battle. He was very much proud of his physical strength. Kanhoji Jedhe was the most respected among the Deshmukhs of the area but he was a strong enemy of Afzal Khan and a supporter of Shivaji. The Deshmukh of Khopde had enmity with Kanhoji so he went to support Afzal Khan. He vowed before Afzal Khan that he would help him arrest Shivaji. Afzal Khan wanted only that Shivaji should get out of the fort. He ordered his soldiers to scatter and hide in the plains around the fort and to arrest Shivaji as soon as he came out of the fort.

A very clever spy of Shivaji, Nanaji Nayak, kept on wandering in the Afzal Khan's camp in the disguise of a Muslim *faqueer* blessing people and begging and passed on the information of Khan's all plans to Shivaji. Knowing about the true intention of Afzal Khan he made a sound arrangement of his security. He hid specially trained soldiers in the caves of the hill. Afzal Khan was busy making his plans so he could know about Shivaji's plan.

Enthusiasm was a special feature of Shivaji's personality. He was always ready to face any type of hardships but it did not mean that he was careless about the security arrangements. Probably, this was also a strong reason behind his successes. His sharp brain had cautioned him in advance about the security arrangements while meeting Afzal Khan. As per the plan, the base of the Pratapgarh Fort was fixed the meeting place for Shivaji and Khan. A beautiful hut was built there. A beautiful roadway was made for Khan to come. It was specially taken care of that nobody could enter the fort from any side. All the possible ways were blocked with tree-trunks etc. Shivaji told all about his plan to Moropant, Netaji Palkar and Tanaji Malsure. Netaji Palkar was to hide in the eastern side of the fort because it was suspected that Khan's army could come through that side. Moropant went to Jawali behind the Khan's army. Five cannon fires was fixed to be the signal for attack.

Afzal Khan wanted to come fully armed along with 1500 soldiers, but since there was lack of space for so many people at the meeting spot, his arms and number of soldiers were lessened to the minimum. He was told that Shivaji would get frightened from so many arms and soldiers so he should only keep a sword with him. According to the conditions fixed Shivaji could not carry any servant or arm with him. Khan's messenger Krishnaji and Shivaji's messenger Pantaji Gopinath were to be there to assist them in the compromise talks.

Before leaving for the meeting spot, Shivaji told his men to continue with his goals of life even if he died or was captured in the process. He worshipped the family deity, Man Bhawani, and took a little food. He put on the shield made of iron chains under his dress and an iron cap under his turban. He also put the tiger's claw on his hands and hid a small knife within his arm. He got ready, touched his mother's feet, got her blessings and started for the meeting spot.

Afzal Khan had already reached the spot and was getting angry for Shivaji coming late. As per the condition Shivaji reached there with only one servant, Tanaji Malsure. Khan had a more strong built body than Shivaji and was older by 20 years in age. Perhaps Shivaji stopped short of Khan having a look of his physical strength. Khan sent his bodyguard a little far on seeing that Shivaji was frightened. The messengers introduced Khan and Shivaji. Khan stood up from his seat and embraced Shivaji. (According to Indian historians) He held Shivaji by neck with his left hand as he wanted to draw his sword with the right hand. Shivaji tore his stomach with the tiger's claw and pulled the intestine out.

After this Khan's bodyguard come forward to fight but was killed. The palanquin bearers tried to take Khan's dead body away but they were attacked. They were injured and Khan's head was chopped off. Both the messengers were stunned at this sight. Khan's head was hanged from the tower of the fort. The Maratha soldiers came out of their hidings and killed the Bijapur soldiers whom they saw on their way. Shivaji did not do anything to those who surrendered, but the others were killed. Many of the Bijapur soldiers accepted Shivaji's service. Many were lost in the jungles.

The next day the Maratha army attacked the main Bijapur soldiers' camp at Bai. More than half of the Bijapur army was there under the control of Afzal Khan's son Fazal Khan. Here also the Marathas won. Fazal Khan fled away but his two brothers, many *samants* and soldiers were arrested.

After surrendering, the soldiers who wanted to return to Bijapur were given valuable gifts and sent away with respect. The sons of Afzal Khan and other important *samants* were under the care of Khanduji Kakare. He had become ready to leave them upto Kurar through secret hill paths in return for a hefty amount of bribe. Shivaji got this information and chopped off his head as a punishment.

Panhala Encounter

After the death of Afzal Khan Shivaji captured the small forts of Panhala, Khelana, Rangana and Vasantgarh etc. In fact this victory was not a permanent victory, but the beginning of his long struggle with Bijapur. Khelana was renamed Vishalgarh. The fort of Vishalgarh had been under Rustame Zama for quite a long period. As soon as Shivaji captured the fort, he fled away and Fazal Khan also succeeded in fleeing away so they both jointly attacked Panhala. Shivaji defeated them on 28th of December, 1659 and drove them away upto Bijapur. That time Netaji Palkar and other Maratha commanders looted the cities around Rambagh, Gadak and Lakshmeshwar etc. Shivaji reached Ramgarh in January 1660 with the looted wealth.

In Bijapur, there was again a discussion on how to suppress Shivaji. For this Siddi Jauhar, the officer in Karnul province, was summoned. Giving the title of *Salawat Khan* he was sent to attack on Panhala along with Baji Ghorpare, Rustame Zama and Fazal Khan etc. Siddi of Janjira and the *samant* of Bari were also sent to fight against Shivaji. Their huge army surrounded the Panhala Fort. Shivaji himself took the command of his army from the Panhala Fort to encounter them. A fierce battle ensued in May, 1660. Shivaji handed over the charge of protecting the fort on Kadtoji Gujar and Netaji Palkar remained outside to check the military and food supply of the enemy. Salawat Khan was a skilled commander. He attacked with full force and so Shivaji fell weak. Mata Jijabai got the news in Rajgarh. She ordered Netaji Palkar to intensify the battle in order to protect Shivaji.

Salawat Khan asked the British traders of Rajapur to help him. Hence, the chief officer of the ammunition factory Riwington along with two assistants, Mingham and Giffard, reached from Rajapur with heavy cannons and arms and ammunitions. This made Shivaji's situation quite insecure.

At the same time Shivaji had to face one more problem. Shaista Khan had come as the Mughal governor of south in February 1660. As soon as he reached Ahmadnagar, he captured Shivaji's forts of Poona, Bharamati, Shikhal and Chakan. After capturing Poona he started living in Shivaji's Lalmahal. It was a very difficult situation for Shivaji but he did not lose courage. He sent his minister Sonopant Dabir to Shaista Khan to persuade him for a compromise and to help Shivaji. Khan was ready for this because he knew that it would be very difficult for his army to fight a battle in the hills of Maharashtra. So, he sent his men to Delhi to seek advice from Aurangzeb, but Aurangzeb advised him not to do so, and to let the battle continue and finish Shivaji. Raja Jai Singh was ordered to fight against Shivaji from Gujrat in order to help Shaista Khan.

After this Shivaji used a new trick. He sent a message to Salawat Khan that he was ready to compromise. Salawat Khan agreed to it. He ordered a temporary ceasefire. It was raining cats and dogs on the 13th of July, 1660 in the complete dark night. Taking it as appropriate time, Shivaji, along with his most affectionate Bajiprabhu Deshpande and some other bodyguards fled towards Vishalgarh through the backdoor of the fort. The enemies very soon knew it. So a troop began to chase. They were chasing so fast that it became difficult for Shivaji to enter the fort. Bajiprabhu stopped with a few soldiers at the mouth of the narrow mountain pass, Ghorkhind, which was the eastern gate of the fort. He countered the Bijapur troop very bravely, though he was outnumbered. All of them were killed one by one, but by then Shivaji had entered the fort very safely. The sacrifice of life of Bajiprabhu saved Shivaji's life. There are very few such examples of sacrifice in the history. The encounter of Panhala continued for four months, but they could not get Shivaji. Now, it had been very necessary for Shivaji to counter Shaista Khan as the Mughal empire was a greater enemy than Bijapur. So, he compromised with Bijapur to hand them over the fort of Panhala on 22nd Sept. 1660.

Four

Ups and Downs

Aurangzeb went to the north from Aurangabad on 25th of January 1658 when he heard of the illness of Shahjehan and in July he put his father into the prison and declared himself the emperor. The humiliating murder of Darashikoh and the treatment he meted out to his two brothers have another history. It is not necessary to mention them in this context. As soon as he occupied the throne he sent his maternal uncle Shaista Khan to south as governor and ordered him to crush Shivaji. Shaista Khan reached Aurangabad in January, 1660 and started his anti-Shivaji activities.

Encounter with the Mughal Army and Victory

Shivaji fled from Panhala and reached Vishalgarh, but by then Shaista Khan had already captured many of Shivaji's forts and had started living in his Lalmahal. This all we have read in the earlier chapter. Soon Shivaji reached Rajgarh from Vishalgarh. Now he had to stop Shaista Khan's activities. Since Shivaji got both food grains and wealth from Kalyan, Shaista Khan wanted to finish his rule from this area. He sent a huge army under commander Kartbal Khan for the purpose. Kartabal Khan started from Poona in January 1661. He wanted to go to the downside of Lohgarh through the Umberkhind mountain pass of the Western Ghats. This pass is about eight miles in length. It is so narrow that not more than two persons can walk side by side and also there was no water in between this eight miles length. This pass proved to be very troublesome for the Mughal army, but the Marathas had spent their whole life in these mountains and passes so it was not difficult for them to fight a battle here. Shivaji had got this information from his spies so he decided to defeat the enemy in this pass only. His trained soldiers hid on the way. The Mughal army did not know this. The whole army climbed down into the pass with all food and arms and ammunitions. Suddenly the Maratha army closed the mouths of the pass on both the ends and started bombardment. The Mughal army did not get any way to escape. They started dying of thirst and suffocation.

There was a woman soldier in the Mughal army who was Brahmin by caste and was the wife of Wasim's *samant* Udaram. Kartabal Khan sent this lady to Shivaji to request for mercy. The Marathas took heavy penalty from the Mughal army and then opened the mouth of the pass. The Mughal army cut a sorry figure and returned to Poona.

Revenge on the Britishers

After humiliating Kartabal Khan Shivaji deputed Netaji Palkar to watch the activities of the Mughals and he himself went towards Rajapur. The British traders had helped the Bijapur army in Panhala so he had to take revenge on them. In the beginning of 1661 he attacked the Bijapur provinces, captured Konkan, robbed Nizampur and snatched away Dalvi from them. After that he reached the famous seaport Sangameshwar, worshipping Bhagwan Parsuram in Chiploonkar on the way. He handed over this province to Tanaji Malsure and Pilaji Neelkanth and he himself went to Rajapur. Rewington, Mingham, Giffard and their interpreter Valji had come to help Salawat Khan at the time of Panhala encounter. Earlier Shivaji had warned them that they were traders, so they should not indulge themselves in internal battles but they did not pay attention to his words and took part in the battle against him. Hence, when he reached Rajapur, he summoned the traders to meet him. The chief officer of the factory fled away. Others came very happily to meet him out of which six—Randulf Taylor, Richard Taylor, Giffard, Feyrond, Richard Napier and Samuel Bernard—were arrested and their factory was robbed. The captive traders were kept in Bhasotagarh and Songarh. Shivaji appointed Raoji Somnath to look after Rajapur and also the prisoners. They were well taken care of. A few days later Raoji Somnath put a proposal before the British prisoners that if they agreed to support Shivaji in his campaign against Siddis of Janjira, they would be freed and also their loss would be made up. And if they didn't agree to it then they would have to pay money for their release. The traders refused this proposal. They wrote letters to their chief officer in Surat and requested him to get them released by paying the money, but in vain. They got the reply from Surat, "You very well know why you have been imprisoned. You took part in the war and bombardement from under that flag which is known as the Royal British Flag. Shivaji has only done what any capable person should do. So, you harvest what you have sown."

At last these prisoners begged for mercy from Raoji Somnath. One of them had been sick so he was released, though he died within a year. The other prisoners were also released in January 1663 with the permission of Shivaji, but before the release they had to take this oath, "We would not repeat such deeds in future."

When Shivaji appointed Raoji Somnath the administrator of Rajapur, he got the information that the *samants* of Sringarpur had defeated his representative, Tanaji Malsure, and had arrested him in Sangameshwar. Shivaji immediately rushed to Sringarpur. As soon as Suryarao Surwe heard of Shivaji's arrival, he fled away from Sringarpur, so Sringarpur came easily under Shivaji's rule. This province was spread from Sangameshwar to Dapoli. Shivaji built new forts here also and kept Trayambak Bhaskar to manage them.

Attack on Shaista Khan

After the defeat of Kartabal Khan Shaista Khan sent a huge army and captured the regions around Kalyan and Pane. The next year Shaista Khan sent Namdar Khan to attack Pane. There the army of Shivaji defeated him.

Shaista Khan was stationed in Poona and his spies gave him information of each of Shivaji's activities. Shaista Khan knew that Shivaji was very clever so he took special care of the security arrangements in Poona. No armed Maratha could enter Poona without a permission letter. Shivaji also knew Shaista Khan's activities. So, he decided to give a surprising challenge not only to Shaista Khan but also to the Mughal empire. He reached Singhgarh to carry out his plan.

Shivaji sent two Brahmins to Poona who took the permission for a marriage procession in the city with the help of a Maratha soldier in Shaista Khan's army. Shivaji divided four hundred brave Mawale soldiers in groups of 25 and sent them into the city in the disguise of the Mughal soldiers. Those days many new soldiers were included in the Mughal army so they were hardly noticeable. Entering the city they all joined the marriage procession. It was the month of *Ramzan* so Shaista Khan and his family took supper early and slept. The moon had hidden. Only a few earthen lamps were glowing. In such a night on 5th of April, 1663 Shivaji, along with fifty soldiers, broke into Shaista Khan's house. The Maratha soldiers started killing the men and women sleeping inside. Shaista Khan jumped out of a window but the sword cut his fingers. One of his sons, Abdul Fatah Khan, was killed. An officer and six women were also killed. Two of Shaista Khan's sons and eight maid servants were injured.

After all this Marathas fled away in a few moments. Some Maratha soldiers were also killed during their escape, but Shivaji was able to reach the Singhgarh fort safely. Next day the Mughal army attacked the Singhgarh fort but they had to retreat due to the superior artillery of Shivaji.

Shivaji had achieved the impossible through this attack. This earned him a big reputation. The rainy season was approaching so Shaista Khan decided not to attack Shivaji again that time. He went back to Aurangabad as he thought that he was not safe in Poona. Aurangzeb removed him from there being angry with his defeat. After that Raja Jai Singh was sent to suppress Shivaji in 1664.

Loot in Surat

Of course, the attack on Shaista Khan in Poona was a courageous work, but it did not gave much benefit to Shivaji's state. Now, Shivaji raised a huge army and pretended that it was with the purpose of combating the Mughals. One of his spies, Baddhirji, had informed him that he could get a lot of wealth if he looted Surat. Those days Surat was the main centre of sea trade. This was the port from where the Haj pilgrims went to Mecca. There were minimum twenty multi-millionaire traders out of whom two or three were counted among the richest in the world. Mulla Abdul Zafar had nineteen ships full of valuable trade items.

Surat was at a distance of about two hundred miles from

Shivaji's present dwelling. Going there or keeping up-to-date communication was difficult. So first he set up two army camps near Danda Rajapuri and Pune and told the people that it was to suppress the Siddis and the Portuguese. This army of four thousand soldiers started from Nasik on first January 1664 in parts and reached Gandevi, 21 miles from Surat on the 5th of January.

The people in Surat were terrified when they heard of the army coming nearer. Many of them fled away with bag and baggage. A message was sent to the governor of Surat, Inayatullah Khan that Shivaji required money as he was fighting against the Mughal emperor. This money should be collected from the traders.

Shivaji wanted fifty lakh rupees which the traders could easily have given collectively. So, another message for the traders was sent: "Tomorrow we will be in Surat. You all meet us and give in written that you would give money. If you fail, we will adopt some other hard steps and you will be responsible for that."

None paid attention to Shivaji's warning. The messenger was arrested. Next day Shivaji entered the city at 11:00 a.m. The governor fled away. The soldiers collected money from the traders as much as possible. Next day, on 7th January the governor sent a messenger to Shivaji with peace proposal. He wanted to meet Shivaji alone. When they met in a lonely place, he attacked Shivaji with a dagger but was killed. Now Shivaji's bodyguards and the soldiers wanted a massacre in Surat, but Shivaji did not allow. Yes, hands were cut off of those who had conspired. All the rich people of the city were robbed and their houses were set on fire. Almost two-thirds of Surat was ruined but nobody opposed. The Christians were not disturbed because their main priest had already asked for pardon.

On 9th January Shivaji got the information that a large Mughal army was coming to protect Surat. Hence, he returned with all the valuables. Probably the total loot was more than one crore which was sent to the Raigarh Fort.

Only a few days later he got the news that his father had fallen down from the horse and had died while chasing a deer on 23rd January 1664.

Humiliation of Bijapur

After the enclosure of Panhala there was a compromise between Shivaji and Bijapur and the Panhala fort was returned to Bijapur. The Shah of Bijapur pitched his camp in Bankapur in order to capture Konkan under the pretention of Karnataka campaign in the beginning of 1663. At that time Konkan was under Shivaji. At the information of the Shah of Bijapur's arrival the *samant* of the region, the Dutch traders of Birgula and the Portugese traders of Goa were afraid. Shivaji's stepbrother Ekoji also marched against Shivaji. Shivaji had got this information, so he was well prepared. One by one he defeated all of them. He suddenly attacked Mudhol which was under his cousin Baji Ghorpare, deadly enemy of Shivaji. He had played the key role in 1648 when Shahji was arrested. This time in 1664 he was killed along with many of his soldiers fighting against Shivaji. Shivaji got a lot of wealth from here. Capturing Mudhol he made Maloji Ghorpare, the youngest son of Baji Ghorpare, the samant there.

After Mudhol he faced Khawas Khan who was in Khanapur then. Khawas Khan and his 200 soldiers were killed in this battle. After this he robbed Khanapur, Hubli etc. Meanwhile the samant of Kudal went into the camp of Bijapur. So, to punish him Shivaji robbed his province and captured it. The samant was given shelter by the Portuguese, therefore their Poda Fort was exploded. At this the Portuguese begged for mercy and presented many cannons as gift. A messenger of the samant came to Shivaji to have a talk and Shivaji returned half of his state to him.

Shivaji's stepbrother Ekoji had also fought in support of Bijapur for which the Sultan had honoured him and given him awards. Shivaji avenged for all these later.

Face-to-face with Jai Singh

The Mughal emperor, Aurangzeb, was alarmed at the growing influence of Shivaji. Earlier he took him only as a 'hill-rat' or a 'dacoit', but the way he defeated Shaista Khan forced him to change his opinion. So he sent Raja Jai Singh to suppress him. The Surat loot had angered him even more. Diler Khan and Raja Jai Singh were the most competent and trustworthy to the emperor. Jai Singh was honoured as a prince in the court of the Mughal emperor. The emperor was very much influenced by his political skill and warfare.

On 30th September 1664, on the occasion of his birth anniversary, Aurangzeb honoured Jai Singh with special clothes and sent him against Shivaji. Jai Singh left for South with a big army along with Diler Khan, Daud Khan and his son Kirat Singh and reached Buharanpur on 19th January 1665. After making preparations for a few days he reached Aurangabad on 10th February and Poona on 3rd March. At that time Shivaji was at the coast of Kanara so he returned from Poona. He had arranged that Bijapur should not help Shivaji. *Samant* of Kudal again went against Shivaji. The emperor had ordered Jai Singh to chase Shivaji in Konkan but the hilly area was very difficult for the Mughal army to pass. He captured the plateau region between Lohgarh and Rajgarh and all the provinces neighbouring Poona. After that he called the Europeans along with naval force from both Bombay and Goa. He also sent messengers to all the *samants* of Karnataka. Afzal Khan's son Fazal Khan and the lord of Bednoor also joined Jai Singh. The emperor had given Jai Singh permission to spend as much as he thought proper for the work. The monsoon was approaching so he made the main camp of his army in Sasawgarh and his own temporary dwelling in Poona. He placed seven thousand soldiers in Lohgarh under the supervision of Kutubuddin Khan for the protection of the western mountain pass.

Jai Singh used diplomacy too along with the military preparations. He deputed messengers to convince Shivaji that the emperor was neither opposed to Hindu nor to Shivaji so he should willingly accept the subordination of the Mughal empire.

In the end of March Jai Singh went to Sasawgarh from Poona and ordered Diler Khan to surround Purandar Fort. There was treasury also in the fort of Rajgarh. Daud Khan Quraishi was sent to capture Rajgarh. The security guards of Vajragarh, which were near Purandar, themselves proposed to accept the Mughal rule. Shivaji sent Netaji Palkar to capture Parenda but he failed. It is said that Jai Singh had bribed Netaji and so he marched much ahead of Parenda along with his cavaliers, though there is no such mention in the Maratha record.

Diler Khan attacked Purandar on 30th March. Though

fort custodian Murarbaji used his guerilla war to starve the enemy and put their arms and ammunitions on fire but could not defeat the big Mughal army. Diler Khan captured Rudramal which was below Purandar. The brave Murarbaji continued to fight even when his hands were cut but finally he was killed. Even then the enemy could not enter the fort.

Jai Singh continued to send his proposal to Shivaji from time to time. Shivaji was compelled to accept the proposal by his miserable condition. Shivaji along with six Brahmins went into the camp of Jai Singh on 11th June 1665. Diler Khan was in Purandar itself when these two were on the talks. On the insistence of Jai Singh Shivaji went to meet Diler Khan at his residence alone and completely unarmed on the 12th June. Actually Jai Singh wanted Diler Khan to take initiative in the matter because he was a Muslim so the emperor had more trust on him. Diler Khan was very happy with Shivaji's behaviour. He gave him two horses, a sword, a jewelled *katar* and some clothes as gift. He tied the sword on Shivaji's waist with his own hands.

Shivaji stayed in the Mughal camp for four days. Shivaji, Jai Singh and Diler Khan jointly fixed the conditions for the treaty. He returned on 15th June to hand them over the forts as per the treaty. The main conditions of the treaty were:

(1) 23 forts of Shivaji and area earning four lakh Hones should be handed over to the Mughal empire. Shivaji will rule over the remaining 12 forts and area earning one lakh Hones as an employee of the Mughal emperor.

(2) Shivaji's son Sambhaji will remain in the Mughal court as a five-thousand strong *Mansabdar*.

(3) Shivaji will have the right to collect *chauth* (one quarter) from two of the neightbouring states.

Jai Singh's son, Kirat Singh, accompanied Shivaji when he returned from the Mughal camp. He gave the keys of all the 23 forts to Kirat Singh who went back to Jai Singh on 19th June. Jai Singh sent a detailed description of the treaty to Aurangzeb who became very happy. He sent an order with the impression of his palm and a pair of *khilat* for Shivaji. These reached Jai Singh's camp on 30th of September. According to the conditions of the treaty Shivaji could not put on any arm for three months as a punishment for conspiring against the Mughal rule. But when Aurangzeb's order reached there Jai Singh himself gifted him a jewelled sword.

Attack on Bijapur in Favour of the Mughals

According to another condition of the treaty Shivaji fought against Bijapur in favour of the Mughals. This battle started on the 20th of November 1665 and passed through many ups and downs. Shivaji' army lost at many battles after being very close to victory. For this Diler Khan heaped all the blames on Shivaji and insisted that he should be killed. Earlier also at the time of attack on Purandar he talked the same. Jai Singh found it very difficult to save Shivaji's life in these conditions. Hence, in the mid January he sent Shivaji to attack the south western province of Bijapur. Here also the army of Bijapur was ready to face him. They countered the Marathas very bravely. One thousand Maratha soldiers died in a fierce battle. In the meantime it was dawn. The Maratha soldiers who were trying to climb the fort became visible. The Bijapur army shelled heavily and the Maratha army was finally defeated so Shivaji went to the fort of Khelana, about 28 miles away.

There arose a serious conflict between Shivaji and his trustworthy commander, Netaji Palkar. The reason for the conflict is not known. Netaji had left Shivaji's service when he was fighting against Bijapur in favour of the Mughal and accepted the service of the Bijapur kingdom. Later Jai Singh sent him in the service of the Mughal emperor.

After this Shivaji started preparations to go to Aurangzeb to follow the conditions of the treaty.

Five

Lion in the Cage

Shivaji did not have full faith in Aurangzeb but Jai Singh had the confidence that he would be able to bring a permanent compromise between the two. Shivaji had taken care that he had sent his son to the Mughal court in spite of going himself. But according to the conditions of the treaty he personally had to go to the emperor at least once. Jai Singh and his elder son Ram Singh both took full responsibility of his safety in Delhi. They gave Shivaji a written bond.

Shivaji had shown good heroism during the war against Bijapur and the Mughal army had won so Aurangzeb had given him gifts also. He had also written a letter to Shivaji on 5th of April 1666 in which he had invited Shivaji to come over to Delhi and had assured him that he would get proper respect in the court and would be given a higher post, after that if he wished he would be free to go back to south. The emperor had also sanctioned Rs. One lakh for the expenses on his journey from Rajgarh to Delhi. He had ordered his men to honour him like a prince.

Finally, Shivaji became ready to go to Agra. It is notable that Aurangzeb was in Agra at that time so the capital also was there only. Shivaji sent Raghunath Pant to inform the emperor that Shivaji was going to Agra. Probably he wanted to know what was going on in the Mughal court about him. Jai Singh had also sent the information to the emperor about Shivaji's arrival in Agra.

Before he left Rajgarh, Shivaji had made all the arrangements about how the administration would go during his absence. He gathered all his officers and in their presence declared that Mata Jijabai would be the head of the administration and Moropant Peshwa, Nilopant Mazumdar and Prataprao Gujar were made the members of working administration committee. After that he toured all the regions which were under him. He told all the local officers and the security guards of the forts to remain careful and to obey Mata Jijabai in his absence. After making all these arrangements he left for Agra form Rajgarh on 5th March, 1666. At that time his son Sambhaji, some important officers, some servants and four thousand bodyguards were with him.

Shivaji got a letter from Aurangzeb on the way on 5th April in which he had expressed his pleasure on Shivaji's departure from Rajgarh. He had written, "Your letter in which you have written that you have started for Agrea has been produced before me. Have full faith in me and come to me peacefully without any delay. You will be overwhelmed seeing the royal hospitality when you reach here and you will get permission to go back home. I am sending a splendid *Khilbat* to you."

When he reached Aurangabad, people came to see him but the governor, Safshikan Khan did not turn up to welcome him. Shivaji took it as his insult, so he went straight to Jai Singh's camp. Jai Singh scolded Safshikan Khan for this and condemned his behaviour. The very next day Safshikan Khan met Shivaji and Shivaji got statisfied. Next day when Shivaji was returning he went to Safshikan Khan to see him and marched towards north.

Agra was very dear to Shahjehan. When Aurangzeb took the empire in his hand in 1658, he imprisoned Shahjehan in Agra but did not enter Agra for eight years till Shahjehan was alive. He came to Agra only after Shahjehan's death on the 22nd of January 1666. 12th or 13th of May was his 50th birth anniversary so he wanted to sit on the '*Mayur Singhasan*' for the first time on this day only. Very recently he had got rid of a long illness. All his enemies had been silenced by that time. So, it was fixed that Shivaji would meet him on that day only.

Meeting with Aurangzeb

Shivaji reached Sarai Malukchand after a tiring journey of five hundred miles in two months on the fixed day. There was a common rule of the court that if any important person came to meet the emperor, one or two *Umrao* of the court were sent to great him. This duty was assigned to Jai Singh's son

Ram Singh but that day it was his turn to guard the fort, so he could not go to greet Shivaji. Instead he sent his representative, Munshi Girdhari Lal. Girdhari Lal lost the way and brought them by a long path so Shivaji was delayed. Then Ram Singh reached Noorganj Bagh to receive him. Here Taj Singh introduced Shivaji and Ram Singh to each other. After that Mukhlish Khan met him. Shivaji was not honoured properly as Ram Singh was only a simple Mansabdar in the court. Shivaji felt the pang of insult for the first time here.

From there Ram Singh first took him to his residence where Shivaji was properly honoured. Then Ram Singh and Mukhlish Khan took him to the court. The functions of the Diwan-e-Aam had been over by then and the emperor had gone into the Diwan-e-Khaas so, Shivaji was also taken there. The Diwan-e-Khaas, made of white marble, was decorated that day in a special manner. Valuable carpets were laid on the floor. The emperor was sitting on the throne. All lower and higher *samants* were standing according to their cadre. There colourful clothes doubled the glory of Diwan-e-Khaas.

On the emperor's order Bakhshi Asad Khan took Shivaji before him. One thousand gold coins, two thousand rupees as gift from Shivaji and five thousand rupees as propitiatory offering were presented before the emperor's feet. Sambhaji was also introduced to the emperor. From his side one hundred gold coins, one thousand rupees as gift and two thousand rupees as propitiatory offering were presented, but the emperor did not speak even a word to Shivaji. He was forced to stand with five-thousand-strong *Mansabdars*. The proceedings of the court continued. After that the princes and the *samants* were given *Pan* but Shivaji was overlooked. Shivaji felt as if he won't get the honour he had hoped of. Prince Wazir Zafar Khan and Yashwant Singh, the king of Jodhpur, were given *Siropao*, but Shivaji was deprived of this also and he was made to stand for an hour. He could not tolerate all this. His face started showing reaction. The emperor marked it and said to Ram Singh, "Ask Shivaji, what problem does he have!" Ram Singh came to Shivaji and repeated the question. Shivaji said, "You have seen, your emperor has seen. Am I such a person who should be made to stand like this? I am quitting the status of your officer. If you had to keep me standing, at least you should have selected a proper place." Saying so he turned his back on the throne and walked away. Ram Singh held him by his hand, but he gave him a jerk and sat in one corner. Ram Singh tried a lot to persuade him but in vain. Shivaji said, "Either you kill me or I will commit suicide. If you wish, you can chop off my head, but I won't go in the service of your emperor."

Ram Singh narrated all this to the emperor. Then the emperor ordered Multiafit Khan, Aquil Khan and Mukhalish Khan to present Shivaji a *Siropao* and to bring him to the emperor. They went to Shivaji and requested him to go to the emperor putting the *Siropao* on. At this Shivaji said, "I refuse your *Siropao*. The emperor knowingly placed me below Yashwant Singh. Neither I accept his *monsab* nor will of become his servant. If you wish kill me or imprison me. But I won't put on your *Siropao*."

The three *samants* narrated the whole episode to the emperor. The emperor ordered Ram Singh to take Shivaji with him and try to persuade him. Ram Singh took him to his own residence. He tried a lot to convince him but Shivaji was not ready to listen to him.

There were some anti-Shivaji *samants* in the court. They tried a lot to instigate the emperor against Shivaji's behaviour.

It was a great problem for the emperor. He was not able to decide what action should be taken against Shivaji. One of his *begams*, one *sardar* who was opposed to Jai Singh and one or two courtiers poisoned his ears that Shivaji was a very small country landlord. He had insulted the emperor in the open court. If he was not punished, others could also do the same. Ram Singh was not leaving any stone unturned in order to persuade Shivaji. Next day Ram Singh appeared in the court alongwith Sambhaji. The emperor gave him complete clothes, a jewelled dagger (*Katar*) and a pearl-necklace, but even this could not pacify Shivaji.

Imprisonment of Shivaji

Till 2-3 days everybody had the hope that Shivaji would calm down and would go to the court to apologise for his action but nothing like this happened. So, Aurangzeb decided that either he would imprison Shivaji or kill him. Before giving him death sentence he found it necessary to ask Jai Singh about the promises he had made to Shivaji, but it would take time as Jai Singh was in south then. So he decided to keep

Shivaji interned at the residence of Raudaiz Khan, the guard of the Agra Fort till any reply came from Jai Singh. When Ram Singh got this information he sent this message to the emperor through minister Aamin Khan, "Shivaji has come here on the assurances from me and my father. The security of his life is my responsibility. Hence, the emperor should kill me before doing any harm to Shivaji." At this rigidity of Ram Singh the emperor got a personal bond signed by him that it would be his responsibility if Shivaji committed suicide or escaped. Ram Singh did it but still Aurangzeb was not satisfied. He ordered the officer-in-charge of Agra to deploy military at the residence of Shivaji. Cannons were fixed on all the sides. Some soldiers and officers of the Amber army were deploed to watch inside. What a pity! He who took an oath of an independent empire and who came to Agra on the assurance of Raja Jai Singh was insulted and imprisoned here. Free roaming lion was put into a cage!

Life in the Prison and Efforts for Freedom

The control over Shivaji became harder with the passage of time. Shivaji was repenting for coming to Agra because he was a prisoner. He was feeling like crying at his helplessness. On the other hand it was a big problem for Aurangzeb too. Both of them were feeling restless about the solution of this problem. Aurangzeb wanted to kill him but in an easy and legal process. Shivaji also knew very well what was to be done to him ultimately, but he was an optimist. So he did not lose courage because he knew, losing courage is timidity and that great people got rid of their harships through courage only.

One day it was planned in the emperor's court that Shivaji should be sent to Kabul under the mastership of Ram Singh but was later cancelled. Shivaji was sure that he could be killed any moment so he decided to draw a few people of the court in his favour. For this he gave money to Zafar Khan who was *wazir* (minister) and some money to a few other courtiers also. He also sent gifts to many of the *samants*. On 20th May Zafar Khan put up Shivaji's prayer before the emperor so his death sentence was cancelled that time.

After this Shivaji sent one more request letter to Aurangzeb in which he wrote, "Your majesty, please permit me to go back to south. I will hand over all other forts of mine also to you. I am a true loyalist. Presently your army is in war against Bijapur. I will fight from your side. My son will remain in your service. It is necessary for me to go to south otherwise the guards of my forts won't obey my letters." But these also cast no effect on Aurangzeb. As a reaction to his letter he said, "It seems as if Shivaji has gone mad. He can't be allowed to go back. Tell him not to meet anyone."

More strict vigilance was set around him after this. Shivaji again wrote to Aurangzeb on the 8th of June, "Please arrange my stay elsewhere. Please don't keep me under Ram Singh." The emperor wrote in reply, "Ram Singh is my true servant. So, you have to live under his control only. His men will also watch you alongwith the army of *kotwal*. Only he will be responsible if you run away or commit suicide." "At this Shivaji told Ram Singh to take back the promise he has made to the emperor. Aurangzeb asked for advice from Jai Singh as to what should be done to Shivaji and cancelled the personal bond signed by Ram Singh. Shivaji sent away most of his servants with the permission of the emperor. The emperor at once sent the permission with Faulad Khan because he wanted least people to stay with Shivaji. So, around 25th July most of Shivaji's servants went to Maharashtra.

Again Shivaji requested the emperor to send him on some pilgrimage so that he could spent the rest of his life as a saint. The emperor laughed cunningly and said, "OK. Let him become a *faqueer* and live in the Allahabad Fort. There my *subedar* Bhadur Khan will watch him well."

Shivaji was very keen regarding his freedom. Probably he wanted least people around him, this was why he sent his men back. Due to such a long stay in Agra and spending on the *samants* and courtiers he had spent all his money so he borrowed sixty six thousand rupees from Ram Singh. Later this amount was paid back to Jai Singh by Shivaji's representative.

Time was passing by and the pressure on Aurangzeb to kill Shivaji was mounting. One of the *Begums* and the emperor's maternal aunt were very much opposed to Shivaji. This maternal aunt of Aurangzeb, who was the wife of Zafar Khan, considered him a devil because of his attack on her brother, Shaista Khan. Once Shivaji had gone to meet Zafar

Khan at his residence but that lady soon sent him back. She had the impression that Shivaji could attack an enemy even if he stood at a distance from him.

In the meantime Aurangzeb got a letter from Jai Singh in which he had written very firmly that no hard action should be taken against Shivaji. Instead his services should be utilized in South. He had requested the emperor to keep his word that he had given to Shivaji on the emperor's behalf. If that promise was broken, not only Jai Singh, but many other Rajput kings will also become the emperor's enemy. Then the emperor gave up the idea of killing Shivaji, but still he wanted to harass Shivaji so much that he should commit suicide. For this, it was necessary to remove him from Ram Singh's neighbourhood. So, a trick was played. The soldiers on guard complained that they are facing trouble in keeping a vigil on Shivaji due to the presence of Ram Singh in the neighbourhood, so Shivaji should be shifted to Fidai Hussain's residence. Shivaji understood the meaning of this shifting very well.

Wonderful Escape

Probably Shivaji had made his plan of escape even before he sent his men away. So, he started pretending as if he had been disillusioned of his life. One day he started to cry embracing Sambhaji. He repeatedly cursed that moment when he had started for Agra. He talked in such a way as if he had lost all hopes of life and if the emperor freed him he would obey all his orders.

Now, probably there were only two servants, Hiroji Furzand and Madari Mehtar, left with him. Shivaji pretended to be ill and lay down on the bed. He completely stopped coming out of the room. He started sending fruits and sweets in large baskets to the Brahmins and saints so that he could get rid of his illness. Every basket was carried hanging by a pole by two palanquin bearers in the evening. In the beginning the *kotwal* and others on watch carefully checked the baskets before letting out, but in the course of time they took it as a regular feature and stopped checking. Shivaji was waiting for this moment only. On the 18th or 19th of August he sent the message to the people on watch that his illness had increased so no one should disturb him. Hiroji Furzand who was Shahji's son born from some maid servant resembled Shivaji a lot. He covered his face and stretched his hand out which wore Shivaji's golden bangle. In the evening both Shivaji and Sambhaji sat in two baskets. Fruits and leaves were laid on them well so that they could not be seen easily. The palanquin bearers carried them. A few baskets were ahead of them and a few were behind. They passed the watchmen undisturbed as usual.

It was a dark night of Bhadrapada. The palanquin bearers put the baskets at a lovely place outside the Agra city, took their rewards and went away. Shivaji and Sambhaji came out of the baskets. Two Maratha servants were with them. All four reached a small village walking six miles in the dark night. There Niraji Raoji was waiting for them with horses. There they divided themselves in two groups. Shivaji took Sambhaji, Niraji, Duttji, Trayambak and Raghav with him and marched towards Mathura and the others went straight away towards Maharashtra.

There, in Agra, when Hiroji alongwith the Maratha servant also left place, there was no activity inside. The watchmen got suspicious and when they checked, they found that Shivaji had escaped, but they could not assess how it was possible. Every officer and soldier on watch was stunned. They searched the whole building but in vain.

Terrified, Faulad Khan reached the emperor with this news. He said, "Your majesty! Shivaji has escaped, but we are nowhere at fault. He was in the room all the time lying on the bed. We kept looking at him very carefully every now and then. We were always there around him. God knows how he escaped. Whether the ground swallowed him or he flew in the sky, none knows."

Aurangzeb became restless. He immediately ordered all his men to arrest those absconders at any cost. The search teams rushed in all the directions. All the ports and the police posts were ordered to check all the southward travellers very minutely and detect Shivaji. Traffic through the passes and bridges were stopped. Ram Singh was blamed that he had helped Shivaji escape and so he was ordered to catch Shivaji. Ram Singh went in the direction of Daulpur to catch Shivaji.

Trayambak Sondeo, Dabeer, Raghunath Ballal, Korde etc. were caught near Agra itself. They were beaten up and forced to give the false statement that Ram Singh had helped Shivaji in his escape. Faulad Khan had also blamed in the same fashion. Hence, in anger, Aurangzeb expelled him from his service and prohibited his entry to the court. Trayambak Sonedeo etc. were given severe inhuman physical torture. They were released on April 1667, six months after Shivaji had reached his place, Rajgarh. Probe was on in the Shivaji escape case for many a day so that they could know the real story of the case. Hence, the people who were on guard at that time were severely punished. Whatever Shivaji had left in Agra was seized.

Ram Singh got pardon after a few days but he could not gain the same honour and trust of the emperor. His father, Jai Singh, also had to face the emperor's anger. Jai Singh had written to his son forbidding to take up the task of guarding Shivaji. The emperor sensed Jai Singh's hand in Shivaji's escape and he was asked to report in the court giving his charge to *shahjada* (prince) Muazzam, the new governor of the south in May, 1667. Old Jai Singh started from Aurangabad. He got a heart-touching shock at such a result of serving a wicked master. He died on way in Buharanpur on 28th May 1667.

Aurangzeb could not forget Shivaji's escape for the whole life. He always repented why he did not get him killed in the beginning. He even wrote in his will, "Ignoring to listen to proper information of the state for even a moment may sometimes cause disastrous results for one has to repent for the whole life. I ignored proper care in keeping that rascal Shivaji. I have to face the consequence till my death."

Instead of going straight to Maharashtra Shivaji went towards Mathura because he was sure there would be strict vigilance on the south-west via Dhaulpur Narwar. Hence he first went to north and then to the east. Thus he was free from any fear of being caught. The first night they rode very fast and reached Mathura. Sambhaji was only nine then so he was tired. It was not possible for him to proceed so soon but it was not possible for Shivaji to stay there either. Three brothers-in-law of Shivaji's Peshwa, Krishnaji, Kashiji and Vishaji, were living in Mathura. Hence Niraji called all three Maratha Brahmins and put their problem before them. They agreed to keep Sambhaji with them. They did not care that they could be punished by Aurangzeb if they were caught. One of the three brothers even accompanied them upto some distance to show them the way.

Shivaji had his hair and beared shaved in Mathura, rubbed ash on his body and proceeded as a saint. Niraji could speak good Hindi so he became the *mahant* (head). Shivaji and others became his disciples. Shivaji had managed sufficient money for the journey. Sticks were made hollow and filled with diamond and gold coins. Rupees were hidden in the shoes. Some gems were put into wax and stitched to their clothes and some were kept in the mouths. They generally travelled in the night and took rest at some lonely place in the day. The saints changed their clothes every day. If they happened to meet somebody on the way, only Niraji talked to him being the leader. On the way Shivaji stopped at the confluence of Ganga and Yamuna in Prayag, took a bath and then again proceeded. At last they reached a village at the bank of Godawari close to the border of Maharashtra. It was evening hence they asked the *Patelin* of the villages for shelter at night. Only a few days ago this village was robbed under the leadership of Anandrao, one of Shivaji's soldiers. As soon as they asked for shelter the *Patelin* stated, "The whole village is empty. Shivaji's men have robbed everything. Shivaji himself is in the prison. It will be better if he dies there only." Saying so she started crying taking the name of Shivaji. Shivaji was strongly feeling like laughing. He ordered Niraji to note down that woman's name and address. Later when Shivaji reached his capital he called that woman and gave her much more than what she had lost.

Reaching Maharashtra

On the 25th day of their start from Agra, probably on 12th or 13th of September 1666, Shivaji's group reached their capital Rajgrah. Reaching the gates they sent the message to Mata Jijabai that a group of saints from north wants to see her. The religious natured Jijabai paid great respect to saints. She came out to see the saints and saluted them. Neeraji, the *Mahant*, blessed her raising his hand, but in the meantime, Shivaji, a disciple of the *Mahant*, appeared from behind and put his head at the mother's feet. Mata Jijabai was much surprised at this behaviour of a saint. Then Shivaji put off the dress of the saint and put his head on her lap. Finding her son near her tears of joy rolled down from her eyes. A very heart-touching sight it was. There was a wave of happiness all around. There was no limit of joy. The safe return of Shivaji was intimated to all other forts through cannon fires. Celebrations were held in the whole of the state. Every now and then there was a cannon fire. Hence, he had to issue a state order that cannons should be fired under limitations and on particular occasions. Many people were rewarded throughout the state.

It has been earlier mentioned that the child Sambhaji was left in Mathura. A false news was aired that he had died on the way to protect him from the Mughals. Hearing this news the Mughals were disappointed. Then Shivaji sent the message to the three Brahmins to come to Maharashtra bag and baggage alongwith Sambhaji. The three brothers dressed Sambhaji as a Brahmin and left Mathura with bag and baggage. At one place on the way a Mughal officer got suspicious.

The Brahmins told him that Sambhaji was also a member of their family, but this also could not remove his doubt. Hence he asked the Brahmins to eat with Sambhaji. About three hundred years ago it was beyond imagination that an orthodox Brahmin family could eat with a person of a low caste, the *shudra*. It was a big religious crisis for the Brahmins. But finally, the dutifulness prevailed and they ate with Sambhaji. Thus Sambhaji was saved. All of them very safely reached Rajgarh.

Later Shivaji honoured the three Brahmins with the title 'Vishwas Rao, a reward of one lakh gold coins and a *jagir* earning fifty thousand rupees per year for their lifelong livelihood.

The extraordinary escape of Shivaji made him a supernatural man in the opinion of the people. In fact even all the means of the all powerful Mughal empire could not keep him in the prison. Now he had to avenge the same Mughal empire, but with care.

Six

Maintenance of Well-Being

The escape and safe reaching home of Shivaji had automatically cancelled the treaty between Shivaji and the Mughal empire through Jai Singh. Hence, for Shivaji it had been important to regain whatever he had lost and to manage their protection, but his strength had lessened as compared to the past. So he had to take any step wisely. Shivaji showed his skill of matured political knowledge in reorganizing his state.

Strength Collection

He had to make very hard labour for 25 continuous days in reaching Rajgarh from Agra. Also there was no sufficient arrangement of proper food in the way. Hence, after reaching Rajgarh Shivaji fell seriously ill twice. Though his soldiers had started to rob the territories in January 1667, he did not think it proper to take up open battle with the Mughals.

Shivaji did not want to do anything against the Mughals then. He put himself in the work of managing his rule in Konkan and at the same time he did not break the treaty forced by Jai Singh. Principlewise he remained a subordinate of the Mughal empire. For this he wrote a letter to Yashwant Singh which read, "The emperor only abandoned me, otherwise, I had the desire that with the permission of the emperor I would win the fort of Kandhar with my own strength and gift it to him. I fled away from Agra only to save my life. Raja Jai Singh was my well-wisher, but he is no more now. You please mediate and request the emperor to pardon me. I shall send my son in the service of the prince (Muazzam) and I will always remain ready with all my military power to help the Mughal empire."

This time, Muazzam, the son of the emperor, was the

governor of the sonth. Jai Singh was given the orders to come back and Yashwant Singh was deputed at his post. Both Prince Muazzam and Yashwant Singh supported this proposal and wrote to the emperor. Aurangzeb accepted this proposal of Shivaji and honoured him with the little of 'Raja'. Shivaji sent his son Sambhaji to Muazzyam in Aurangabad on 4th November who returned after a few days. One army of Shivaji under the leadership of Prataprao and Niraji started working under Muazzam. Sambhaji was given a *jagir* in Barar which was equal to a *mansab* of five thousand by the Mughal empire.

In fact maintaining the Purandar treaty helped Shivaji in protecting his own interests and practically he was not at all harmed in any way. He was a subordinate to the Mughal empire only as a formality. His relation with Bijapur was peaceful and Golkunda also gave him the respect of an independent ruler. The Portuguese also made friends with him. He had already got the right to collect *chowth* from Golkunda and Bijapur through the Purandar treaty and Muazzam also gave it his approval. These two states gave regularly a fixed amount every year (Rs. five lakhs from Golkunda and three lakhs from Bijapur) in order to save themselves from his attack. So, practically these two states were under Shivaji.

This way from 1667 to 1669, Shivaji took advantage of the time as a subordinate of the Mughal empire. During this period he did nothing against the Mughal empire which was the need of time.

Start of War Against the Mughal

Shivaji sounded the bugles of war against the Mughal openly in 1670. In politics nobody is a permanent friend or enemy. So after returning from Agra, Shivaji remained under the Mughal for long three years and kept on increasing his strength and when he felt that he did not require it any more, he started wars against them. He got sufficient reasons for it. It is said that the Mughal governor of the south hated his commander. Diler Khan and Raja Yashwant Singh had become his favourite advisors. Shivaji was also getting close to Muazzam and Diler Khan could not tolerate all these. So he sent a message to Aurangzeb that prince Muazzam with the help of the Marathas was conspiring to become the emperor himself. At this Aurangzeb ordered Muazzam to arrest Shivaji's son Sambhaji and all his commanders, but Muazzam did not do so and signalled them to flee away. Hence, they fled away from Aurangabad in the night itself.

The other reason, as it is said, was that Aurangzeb had sanctioned Rs. one lakh for the expenses on Shivaji's tour to Agra. Later Sambhaji was given a *jagir* in Barar. Aurangzeb seized this *jagir* in order to settle the account of that one lakh rupees. Shivaji took it as his insult. One another reason is said to be Aurangzeb's anti-Hindu policy. He issued an order on the 9th of April 1669, "All the Hindu temples and schools be demolished and all their religious education and traditions be suppressed." He set up a new department in all his states to suppress Hindus. This department was time-to-time asked to submit the progress report. Aurangzeb had a mental deformity that God had made him emperor only to destroy other religions and spread his own. After the death of Shahjehan when he was sure that his emperorship had no hurdles, his mental deformity took a naked form. He started to suppress the Hindus harshly. First of all he ordered the demolition of the famous Vishwanath temple of Kashi on the 4th of December, 1669. The Keshawrao temple of Mathura also met with the same end. He hated the worship of Lord Krishna in Mathura. He changed the name of Mathura into Islamabad. The same was done in Ujjain and Ahmedabad. The Hindu festivals of Holi and Diwali were strictly banned. The temples of Amer, a city in Rajasthan, were demolished in 1680. In his early life also Aurangzeb had been anti-Hindu. When he became the governor of south for the first time, he had converted the famous Chintamani temple in Ahmedabad into a mosque in 1644 slaughtering a cow there.

The news of demolition of the temple of Kashi Vishwanath and constructing a mosque at that site had stirred the Hindus of the whole country. There was havoc in the country. So the protector of the Hindu religion, Shivaji, prepared himself to encounter the Mughals.

The actual reason was that Shivaji was busy increasing his strength during these three years. Now he had the confidence that he could fight the Mughal directly. In the beginning of 1670 he started his campaign robbing Barar. After this he robbed many places in the province of Ausa. Now he had to take back his own forts from them.

Singhgarh was the most important fort among all that he had handed over to the Mughals during the Purandar treaty. It was necessary to capture this fort in order to control the western provinces. Shivaji himself had handed over this fort to Kirat Singh in 1665. This time Udai Bhan Rathor, a very faithful employee of the Mughals, was the custodian of the fort. This fort was naturally secure and also the Mughals had made a very good arrangement for its security. In fact one who had control over this fort, Poona automatically came under his control. Shivaji himself considered this fort to be invincible, but Mata Jijabai expressed her desire that this fort should be captured at any cost and immediately. She was feeling very restless at the news of the demolition of the Kashi Vishwanath temple. She felt as if Shivaji was avoiding to attack taking the fort's invincibility in consideration. So, she invited Shivaji to play the game of dice with her. She put her condition, "If you lose the game, you will have to conquer the Singhgarh fort. I will curse your state if you don't do so." It was impossible for Shivaji to disobey his mother. Mata Jijabai won the game hence it had been compulsory for Shivaji to conquer the fort.

Attacking Singhgarh fort meant to sacrifice some good warriors. The brave warrior Tanaji Malsure went to conquer Singhgarh along with three hundred selected Malwa soldiers at midnight after the rise of the moon on the 4th February 1670. This fort was situated at such a place that no cannons could be fixed to fire on it. It was surrounded by steep hills from all the sides. There was only a narrow path to the main gate of the fort. Reaching there some soldiers hid near the gate under the leadership of Suryaji. Tanaji climbed the wall of the fort with the help of some soldiers. He killed the guard standing there and hurriedly opened the main gate. The soldiers hiding near the gate entered the fort. In the meantime the other guards woke up and rang the siren. The Maratha soldiers started the killing. The Rajputs got up late as they were dead with opium. The Maratha had conquered one portion of the fort. As soon as the Rajput soldiers came nearer, the Maratha soldiers pounced upon them, uttering '*Har Har Mahadev*'. There was a fierce sword fight between Udai Bhan Rathor and Tanaji Malsure. Finally both of them were killed. In order to prevent demoralization of the soldiers Tanaji's brother Suryaji commanded, "Soldiers, my brother has been killed. No problem, you don't get deviated. Now I become your commander." Hearing this the Maratha soldiers started fighting with doubled zeal. About twelve hundred Rajput soldiers were killed. The Maratha army won the battle. They burnt the hay kept in the stable to inform Shivaji of their win.

The next morning the dead body of Tanaji Malsure was brought before Shivaji and Mata Jijabai. Mourning his death Shivaji said, "We got back '*Garh*' (the fort) but lost '*Singh*' (lion for Tanaji)". The Marathas are even today proud of Tanaji's sacrifice. Mata Jijabai called Tulsidas Charan and ordered him to compose poetry mentioning Tanaji's valour.

Capturing Other Forts

Singhgarh was the most important and also it was difficult to conquer it, but Tanaji's sacrifice made it possible. The other forts were not so difficult so Shivaji got freed all those from the Mughals one-by-one. An army was sent to capture Purandar on 8th of March 1670. The army arrested the custodian of the fort, Rajiuddin Khan, and captured the fort. During this campaign only some soldiers attacked Chandwar near Nasik and switched away the royal treasury. Mahali Fort was also attacked but could not be conquered, so Shivaji postponed the idea for the time being. The Maratha army attacked Kalyan on 3rd March 1670. The Mughal governor, Uzbeg Khan, was killed so both Kalyan and Bhiwandi came under the control of the Marathas. Thus Manohar Das, the custodian of the Mawali Fort, lost his supporter, Uzbeg Khan and found himself helpless, so he surrendered the fort to the Maratha on the 16th of June. Thus the whole of the Northern Konkan came under Shivaji. Marathas attacked Junnar, Parendi, Ahmadnagar etc at the end of April 1670 and imposed heavy taxes on them. The Mughals could do nothing against it.

The Second Loot in Surat

In order to challenge Aurangzeb Shivaji planned the second loot in Surat. He got the information that the governor of Surat had died, the security arrangement was also not sufficient. Hence, he started for Surat alongwith selected fifteen thousand cavalier soldiers on 3rd of October 1670.

The people of Surat had got the news in advance so the Indian traders and government employees had already left the city. A wall had been constructed all around the city after the first loot in 1644, but the wall was very weak, Three hundred incompetent soldiers were also employed to protect the city. When they saw the Maratha, they fled away and took shelter in the fort.

The Marathas robbed the city upto their satisfaction for 2-3 days. Almost half of the city had been burnt. The Dutch traders were threatened to keep quiet. They were also assured that none would disturb them. The European traders had already sent their money and valuables to the Suhali port. The French traders pleased the Marathas by giving them valuable gifts. They also tried to rob the British but could not. The Tatar Sarai was in front of the French apartment where the exiled Sultan of Kashgar, who had returned from Mecca, was staying. The Maratha soldiers started firing from behind the trees around the Sarai. The people staying in the Sarai fled away at night. Here the Marathas got the Sultan's entire wealth, a golden bed gifted by Aurangzeb and many valuable articles. The Britishers had fired from their apartment so the Marathas decided to put their apartment on fire. But the Britishers went to Shivaji with a gift of arms and ammunition so Shivaji being pleased with them assured that they would not be disturbed.

They got the news on the third day that a large army was coming from Buharanpur so they left Surat taking sixty six lakh rupees. Before leaving Shivaji wrote a letter to the big traders of Surat that they had to pay Rs. twelve lakh every year to Shivaji otherwise the next year the remaining part of Surat would also be burnt to ashes.

The residents of Surat had become terrified from these two loots. Every now and then there was a rumour of Maratha attack. People started leaving Surat. Very soon this wealthiest port turned into a ruin.

The Battle of Dindori

When Shivaji reached Chandwara on his way back from Surat, he found that the Mughal commander Dawood Khan Quraishi with a large army was waiting for him. Ikhlash Khan was also with him. They attacked Shivaji in the night of 16th

October. Shivaji had sent a part of his army alongwith the wealth looted from Surat through a secret way and the remaining four parts under skilful commanders started fighting against the Mughal army one by one. The Marathas were adopting the peculiar guerilla style. Sometime the Maratha soldiers started riding their horses very fast encircling the Mughal army. A very fierce battle was fought in Dindori. Though the Marathas could not gain much due to the cannons that the Mughal army had, they captured four hundred horses alongwith some soldiers and officers of the Mughal army. The prisoners were released later. A better result of this battle was that the Mughal governor of Dindori came in the service of Shivaji. After this there was no battle between the Marathas and the Mughals for one month.

The Loot in Baglana and Barar

Shivaji attacked Barar, Baglana and Khandesh in the beginning of December, 1670. He also captured some forts. All the villages of Burhanpur, the capital of Khandesh, were looted. This was done under the leadership of his commander Prataprao Gujar. After this the Maratha army attacked the fertile and prosperous province of Barar. Before this the Maratha had never attacked such a far off place. Nobody showed any resistance there. The city of Karanja was looted undisturbed. They gained almost a crore from this loot which was carried on four thousand bullocks and donkeys. All the wealthy people of Karanha were arrested but the wealthiest of them fled away in the disguise of women as he knew that the Maratha soldiers won't touch a woman. The other cities were also looted after this. Whichever Mughal province Shivaji went, he imposed *Chauth.* In fact Shivaji wanted to declare that Maharashtra came under his rule and not of the Mughals. In the end the people of these provinces themselves wrote letters to Shivaji promising to pay one fourth of the earning to him every year.

When Shivaji was in Barar, one Maratha army, under the leadership of Peshwa Moro Trayambak, was robbing the western Khandesh. Hence, Shivaji also went there from Barar. They jointly conquered the fort of Malher on the 5th of January 1671. After this many villages were also robbed conquering many hill-forts like Mulhur, Ghorap etc.

A Meeting with Chhatrasal

Chhatrasal was the son of the famous Champat Rai of Bundela. After the death of Champat Rai he became a simple Mansabdar of the Mughal empire. At the time when Shivaji restarted his fight against the Mughal empire, he was with the Mughal army deputed in south. He suddenly came to Shivaji one day in December 1670. He expressed his desire to fight against Aurangzeb as a commander of Shivaji. In the opinion of Sir Yadunath Sarkar Shivaji trusted only the South Indians. He neither trusted the North Indians nor he could give any post to them. So, in a very polite tone he replied, "O brave man, please go to your province, establish your state there and win the enemy. Most of the people there will support you in the name of your family, so you should fight there. If the Mughals attack you, we will pounce upon them from behind. In this way they will automatically be crushed between the two."

Chhatrasal had not hoped so from Shivaji so he returned unhappy.

The Incidence of Salher

Shivaji had captured the fort of Salher on the 5th of January 1671. He was progressing continuously. His progress had become a big challenge for Aurangzeb. He brought many changes in his policies for South India in order to settle score with Shivaji. He sent the most experienced person, Mahawat Khan, as the chief officer of south in November 1670. The able commander of Gujrat, Bahadur Khan, was sent to assist him. Dawood Khan and Diler Khan were present there in advance. Mahawat Khan, Yashwant Singh, Dawood Khan etc. gathered in Aurangabad in January 1671. They met Prince Muazzam and discussed on how to encounter Shivaji. The Mughal army camped in Parner in the rainy season. The behaviour of the Mughal army at that time showed as they had been indisciplined. The officers were busy with the luxuries like music and dance whereas the petty soldiers were suffering from epidemics. Aurangzeb got this information so he doubted that Mahawat Khan was having some secret agreement with Shivaji. Mahawat Khan was called back from south. The Mughal army had been surrounding the fort of Salher from the time of Mahawat Khan. Now this responsibility of the Mughal army went to Diler Khan and Bahadur Khan. The responsibility of the siege of the Salher fort was given to Ikhalas Khan and Bahadur Khan and Dawood Khan took the charge of stopping the army of Shivaji from coming to help the Salher fort. Bahadur Khan went towards Supe and Diler Khan reached Poona in December 1671. He massacred people in Poona barring children under the age of nine years. Shivaji alongwith many commanders had made the army of Ikhalas Khan miserable from Khandash so Diler Khan had to rush to help Ikhalas Khan. Resultantly the massacre in Poona stopped. There was a fierce fight between the Mughal and Marathas in Salher. The Mughals had to suffer a heavy defeat. Many of their commanders and soldiers were killed and imprisoned. The Marathas also seized all their arms and ammunition. Shivaji immediately made proper security arrangements for the forts of Salher and Khalher.

Bahadur Khan and Diler Khan returned to Ahmadnagar after this defeat. So, the forts of Poona and Nasik came under Shivaji without fighting any further battle. Aurangzeb was very agitated by the defeats. His attention was also diverted to the battle that had started in the Khaiber Pass. He did not even come to the court for three days on hearing the news of defeat in Salher. He said, "It seems as if Allah wants to give the Muslim empire to a non-muslim. Why didn't I die before seeing all this?" Bahadur Khan Koka, the son of the *Dhay Man* of Aurangzeb consoled the depressed emperor and said that he would re-establish the honour of the Mughal in the South humiliating Shivaji. Hence, Mahawat Khan and Prince Muazzam were called back in June 1672 and Bahadur Khan Koka was sent as the chief Mughal administrative officer of South.

Pratap Rao Gujar, a commander of Shivaji, after the Salher win sent a very hard message to the governer, traders and the people of Surat that they send money to the Marathas regularly and should never do any anti-Maratha activity. In reply to this, the governor of Surat also wrote an equally hard language. The Maratha army was busy fighting a battle elsewhere so no action was taken against Surat then.

Shivaji wanted the Mughal emperor to accept him as an independent ruler so he sent Quazi Haider as his messenger to Bahadur Khan and Diler Khan with a compromise proposal.

They sent this information to Aurangzeb but he was opposed to any agreement with Shivaji, so he ordered them to arrest Quazi Haider. He was arrested in Parenda but he successfully escaped from there soon.

Control over Dharampur and Johar

Dharampur and Johar were two small states in the south of Surat towards Bombay. Moro Trayambak, a Peshwa of Shivaji, captured Johar on the 5th of June, 1672. Vikram Shah, the ruler, escaped into the Mughal territory. Only after a few days Dharampur was also won.

In July Peshwa Moro Trayambak started to rob the city of Nasik. Two Mughal officers tried to stop but they had to run away for their life. In October and November the Maratha horse-riders entered Barak and Telangana and started robbing Ramgiri. The Marathas were so skilful in guerilla policy that Bahadur Khan tried a lot but could not catch them. The Mughal army chased them on their return journey so they had to part with some of their looted wealth. There was a small battle between them near Aurangabad in which the Marathas were defeated.

Bahadur Khan and Diler Khan continued to make attempts to suppress Shivaji and regain honour for the Mughal empire. Bahadur Khan shifted the main camp of the Mughal army from Aurangabad to Perpur, to the east of Poona, so that he could control the Poona centre of Shivaji. He also built a fort there in 1672 but got no success.

The Defeat of Shivaneri

Most of the forts of Baglana had come under Shivaji's control but the fort of Shivner, where Shivaji was born, was still under the Mughals. Aurangzeb had deployed Abdul Aziz Khan here who had been converted into a Muslim from a Brahmin. Shivaji had an emotional attachment with this fort. He made all possible efforts to get this fort but in vain. This fort remained with the Mughals till 1755.

Control over Panhala

While attacking the Mughals Shivaji kept on capturing the provinces of Bijapur. Ali Adil Shah, the Sultan of Bijapur, died on 24th November 1672. A four-year-old boy was made the next Sultan. Now the problem was who should be his guardian. There was a difference of opinion among the courtiers. Everywhere there was the sign of mismanagement and revolt. Shivaji was busy in organizing his forts at the moment. Panhala had the same status in the south as Singhgarh in Poona. This fort was handed over to Bijapur a few years ago during an agreement with them. Now Shivaji got a very good opportunity to recapture it. So he made all the preparations to conquer it. Shivaji assembled his army in Rajapur and the Maratha army set out to conquer the Panhala Fort under the leadership of Anaji Dutto. In the dark night of 6th March, 1673 Kondaji Furzand, an assistant of Dutto, climbed the wall of the fort alongwith sixty Mawal soldiers. They pulled up other soldiers and walked towards the top. There they divided themselves into four groups. All the four groups started running within the fort beating drums. The security guards were stunned seeing the enemy inside. There was a big chaos. Kondaji killed the chief security officer of the fort. The treasurer of the fort, Nagoji, fled away leaving everything. Gradually the large Maratha army entered the fort. Before morning the fort was under the control of the Marathas. Shivaji reached the fort on hearing this news. He lived there for one month and made the fort completely invincible and secured. Later he also captured the Sattar and Parli forts of the Bijapur state. The Parli fort was given to Ramdas to build a temple and was renamed Sajjangarh.

The Battle of Umbrani

A commotion was caused in the Bijapur court at the news of Shivaji capturing these forts. Everybody claimed that it was the result of the inactiveness of the new *wazir* (Minister) Khawan Khan. Hence, he sent Bahlol Khan with a large army to conquer Panhala. Three other commanders were sent to his aid with their armies.

Shivaji got this information. He decided to attack Bahlol Khan before he reached Panhala. For this Shivaji sent two commanders, Pratap Rao Gujar and Anand Rao Makaji. Pratap Rao was the commander-in-chief. This army reached Umbrani, about 36 miles away from Bijapur to the west, in two days. Bahlol Khan had camped there. The Marathas surrounded Bahlol Khan's army from all sides. Soldiers started dying of hunger. There was only one way though which they fetched water, that also was blocked on 15th April, 1673. Helpless, they had to come out in the open for the battle. The Bijapur army was very badly defeated.

At this Bahlol Khan requested Pratap Rao for mercy which he accepted and let them run away. It is also said that Bahlol Khan had given a hefty amount to Pratap Rao in bribe and Pratap Rao let them run away. The Maratha army captured whatever was there in the camp.

Sacrifice of Life by Pratap Rao

Shivaji was very angry because his enemy, Bahlol Khan, could run away form Umbrani only due to Pratap Rao's mercy. He did not approve of it. He sent a very hard message to Pratap Rao, "Bahlol Khan has been creating nuisance in our provinces. Go with the arm and unless you arrest him, don't show me your face." Pratap Rao's self-respect got a great shock on hearing such words from Shivaji. He thought in his mind that if he attacked Kolhapur, Bahlol Khan will immediately pounce upon him. So he went and robbed the city of Hubli. Bahlol Khan, as expected, came to face him with all his force. Sarja Khan also came to his help. Pratap Rao got the information that Bahlol Khan was in the village of Nesari at a short distance from the Ghatprabha river which is a few miles to the south from Kolhapur. Immediately he took 7-8 of his bodyguards with him and rode away. The army was left behind. There was only a little mountain pass between them. Pratap Rao pounced upon Bahlol Khan. But Pratap Rao and his seven bodyguards could not stay longer against the large army of Bahlol Khan. They were all killed soon. This happened on 24th February 1674. After this there was a fierce fight between the two armies and unfortunately the Marathas lost the battle. Pratap Rao's sacrifice touched Shivaji. He was sorry for his harsh words for his whole life.

After this Anand Rao rode into Kanara with his cavalry and robbed 7 lakh rupees from Sampgaon, a main point of Bahlol Khan's state. Bahlol Khan attacked him. Both the armies came across at many places. Somewhere the Maratha army dominated and somewhere Bahlol Khan's army. In the end the Marathas were able to carry all the looted wealth to a safe place.

Shivaji inspected his victorious army in Chiploon and rewarded the soldiers. Hansaji Mohite was given the title of '*Hambir Rao*' and made the commander in place of Pratap Rao.

Seven

The Coronation Ceremony

Why Coronation?

Practically Shivaji was an independent ruler now. He had already declared so, but his coronation had not taken place. He was not considered a complete sovereign ruler for this reason. Dr. Yadunath Sarkar writes, "Shivaji conquered many states and collected a lot of wealth, but could not establish himself as *Chhatrapati* or independent king due to which he was facing inconveniences and suffering losses. Some rulers took him to be only a *Zamindar* or *Jagirdar* under Bijapur. Rulers of Bijapur took him to be a rebellious subject. The subjects of Shivaji were also in a dilemma as they were not complied to obey him until he became an independent ruler. Certificates and titles issued by Shivaji were not considered to be authentic."

It feels very odd that in spite of being the master of the whole empire his orders etc. were not considered authentic. But this is a bitter truth that formalities have got their own importance as well as the facts in the social life. In fact Shivaji had also to perform only a formality in order to become an independent ruler. So he decided in favour of coronation. He seeked advices from his well-wishers. He had long discussion with his advisers and concluded that not only the Hindu but the Muslim and other religious sects were also influenced by these rituals. He also wanted to convey the message through this that in true sense he was the owner of his lands.

There were many such Maratha *samants* who could not even imagine an independent state. They were not able to digest the fact that a Maratha was going to become an independent ruler. Till then they considered Shivaji to be a subordinate of Bijapur. It was necessary for Shivaji to put an end to such orthodox thoughts.

Opposed by Orthodox Brahmins

Even though all the ancient religious books, the Vedas and Lord Krishna very clearly declare that the caste system is based on the work, with the passage of time Indian society came under the control of a blunt and orthodox class and with it started the downfall of glorious values of the Hindu culture. The caste system which was formed on the basis of work became on the basis of birth. An illiterate, fool and sinner was called a 'Brahmin' because he had taken birth in a Brahmin family. On the other hand a skilful, competent and virtuous person was barred from the honour he deserved only on the basis of his birth in a lower caste family.

On the occasion of his coronation, Shivaji had also to face such orthodox ideologies. The discussion on coronation had started in the beginning of 1673, but the orthodox Brahmins were not ready to accept Shivaji a Kshatriya. A powerful person who, at such a time when all Hindu kings had surrendered before the Mughals, established an independent Hindu state with his own will power and strength, how he was not a Kshatriya? How could he be denied from claiming to be a Kshatriya when through his deeds he has proved to be one? But the orthodox Maratha Brahmins who were trying to throw *Hindutva* (Hinduism) into the pit were not ready to accept him a Kshatriya. They only argued that according to the Shastras none other than a Kshatriya could be coronated.

The Bhonsles were considered 'Shudras' in the then Maratha society. Though the Bhonsles claimed to be the descendants of the Sisodiya family of Mewar, the Kshatriya culture had vanished from their families. Shivaji was not ready to accept this argument of the orthodox Brahmins. Hence, he sent a delegation of Keshav Chandra Purohit, Bhal Chandra Bhatt and Somenath Bhatt Katre in the leadership of the famous Maratha Brahmin Balaji Aabji to the centres of Kshatriya customs like Udaypur to draw the public opinion in this favour that Kshatriyas still existed. Balaji Aabji was a clever politician and a person who loved his religion and caste. He was quite opposed to the orthodoxy and superstitions spread in the society. The delegation met the

Bhatt Brahmin family of Kashi.

The Bhatt family originally hailed from Paithan of Maharashtra. The famous Brahmin families Kedav, Dharmadhikari, Shesh, Bhatt and Mauni left the ancient cetre of education, Paithan, at the time when Alauddin Khilji attacked South India and took shelter in Benaras. This Bhatt family had so much respect in North India that the presence of at least one member of this family was compulsory at the time of any royal rituals. One of the members of this family, Bishweshwar Bhatt, who had the nickname Gaga Bhatt, was a scholar of his time. He had an immense knowledge of religion, *Puranas*, *Smriti*, politics etc. He had written many a book on these subjects. His books were taken to be authentic even in the then courts. Gaga Bhatt himself was a liberalist and against superstitions. He wrote the book "*Kayastha Dharma Pradeep*" to refute the imaginary principles mentioned in the book '*Shudrachar Shiromani*' written by Krishna Narasingh Shesh. In this book he had proved Kayasthas to be Kshatriyas.

The delegation of Balaji Aawji was very happy to meet Gaga Bhatt. Being influenced by his sharp knowledge he was invited to the coronation of Shivaji. Gaga Bhatt accepted it and issued a certificate that Shivaji was in fact a descendant of the Sisodiya family. So his coronation was in accordance with the *Shastras* as he was a Kshatriya.

Preparation for Coronation

The preparation for the glorious coronation started many a month before the scheduled date. Many important personalities started reaching Rajgarh in palanquins. All the famous Brahmins from all over the country were invited. Though travelling was not safe at that time, almost eleven thousand Brahmin families comprising of about fifty thousand people arrived in Rajgarh. All of them stayed there as Shivaji's guests for four months.

During the first phase of the coronation Shivaji consulted his courtiers, advisers Parmanand, Samarth Ramdas etc. Govind Bhatt Khedkar was sent to escort with respect Gaga Bhatt. Gaga Bhatt reached Rajgarh in time. First of all he had a long consultation with the Brahmins who opposed Shivaji's coronation. He compelled them with his arguments to accept Shivaji as a Kshatriya. Balaji Aawji assisted him in this work.

Coronation was meant to accept Shivaji a Kshatriya. His ancestors had left the customs of the upper caste for many a generation. So his thread ceremony was to take place first. All the requisite items like water from holy rivers, a golden royal throne of appropriate size etc were arranged well in time. Many a temple, pond and building were built.

Elementary Rituals

A few days before the coronation Shivaji had gone on the inspection of Konkan, especially Chiploon. There he met the soldiers and told them to be careful towards their duties. He went to Pratapgarh first on his way back. He worshipped his family deity Tuja Bhawani and offered there a golden royal parasol worth Rs. 56,000. He returned to Rajgarh from there on 21st May.

He touched the feet of his mother Jijabai and his teacher Samarth Swami Ramdas before the elementary rituals. Jijabai was very happy for her long-awaited dream was coming true.

Shivaji's ancestors had left the customs of Rajputs so they were called Shudras. Shivaji made a repentance on the 28th of May. Gaga Bhatt performed the thread ceremony of Shivaji on 29th May, 1674. He made him a Kshatriya by putting the sacred thread around his shoulders. Shivaji said, "Now I have become an upper caste. All upper castes have the righty to the Vedas. The Vedic Mantras should be chanted in all my rituals."

At this the Maratha Brahmins got enraged and said, "The Kshatriya caste has been extinct in Kaliyug. Now there is no upper caste except the 'Brahmin'." Gaga Bhatt also got frightened by such a behaviour of the Brahmins. He very quickly completed the rituals without opposing them.

After the thread ceremony the marriage ceremony of Shivaji with the queen consort Soyarabai was held amongst Vedic chantings.

Coronation Ceremony

Coronation ceremony was scheduled for the 6th of June 1674. One day before that Shivaji lived in full continence. He was given a bath with Ganga water. He gave Rs. twenty five thousand to Gaga Bhatt and Rs five thousand each to the other Brahmins.

On the day of coronation Shivaji got up in the *Brahma Muhurta.* After taking bath he worshipped the family deities Bhawani and Lord Shiva. He then saluted the family teacher Balana Bhatt, Gaga Bhatt and other Brahmins and gave them clothes etc as gifts.

Now, it was the turn of the coronation bath. Shivaji put on white clothes, Sandal necklaces and gold ornaments. He then sat on a gold plated square seat of two feet size. The queen, Soyarabai, sat on his left. Shivaji's mantle was tied to the queen's *sari.* The prince, Sambhaji, also sat near them. As soon as the sacred moment arrived, the eight chiefs poured on them water from holy rivers, oceans and pilgrimages of the country which was stored there in golden tanks. The Brahmins started chanting *mantras*. Sixteen Brahmin women, whose husbands were alive, in beautiful clothes adored Shivaji, the queen and Sambhaji with kindled lamps. Then Shivaji put off the wet clothes and put on embroidered red clothes appropriate for kings. After this he worshipped his sword, *kripan* and other weapons and offered gifts to Brahmins.

In the end he entered the chamber where the royal throne was placed. This grand chamber was very beautifully decorated. An embroidered canopy was fixed with the ceiling. A valuable carpet was laid on the floor. A grand throne, thirteen and a half feet long and twelve feet wide, was placed in the centre. It hand many valuable gems. Its lower part was gold plated whereas the upper one was made of gold. Vessels full of water were placed on either side of the door of the chamber—their mouths covered with green leaves. Two horses and two baby elephants were tied there who had gold chains and gold bridles.

Shivaji sat on the throne at the fixed time. All the eight ministers were standing around him holding the state emblem in their hands. The other officials, guests and invited spectators were standing at their appropriate places behind the ministers. The holy water was sprinkled over Shivaji. Again the sixteen Brahmin women adored him with kindled lamps. The Brahmins were chanting the sacred Vedic hymns. On the occasion many golden lotuses and silver flowers were squandered among the courtiers. The Brahmins blessed Chhatrapati Maharaj Shivaji who accepted the blessings bowing his head. The royal parasol was stretched over Shivaji. Queen Soyarabai also sat with him in the throne. The rituals of coronation finished by eight o'clock in the morning.

Gaga Bhatt was given valuable clothes, ornaments and Rs one lakh on the completion of the coronation rituals. Other Brahmins were given Rs five to twenty five thousand and clothes. Saints, beggars were also given food, money, clothes or gifts.

After the completion of all the rituals. Shivaji talked to the important guests. His chief justice Niraji Raoji brought the British messenger George Oxandon before him. His interpreter Narayan Senoy was also with him. Oxandon presented gifts worth Rs three thousand to Shivaji.

Glory March

After all these the glory march of Shivaji was taken out. This march was headed by two well decorated elephants. Shivaji was on a separate elephant. This march finally reached the Jagadishwar temple moving through the main road of Rajgarh. All the women whose husbands were alive adored Shivaji with kindled lamps on the way. Chhatrapati returned home almost in the afternoon.

Undoubtedly all the Hindus, especially the Marathas, were very happy because of the ceremony. Hindus who had been tortured by the invaders for centuries got new hopes. They had the hope that the future of their religion and culture would be bright. They started sensing a beautiful future of ancient glorious customs. Though Swami Ramdas had presented the saffron flag on the occasion, but it had been in the practice of the Hindu for centuries. The Maratha army used to keep it with them earlier also. The walls, chairs, highways, gates etc were decorated according to the Indian culture.

Total Expenditure on the Occasion

The work of giving away alms to the beggars, *dakshina* to the Brahmins started on the next day of the celebration. This continued for twelve days. The Brahmin women and children also got *dakshina*. Barring the preceptors the total amount paid in *Dakshina* came around seven and a half lakh rupees.

According to Krishnaji Anant the total expenditure on construction works and decoration etc came upto about seven crore ten lakh rupees. The royal throne was made of thirty two pounds of gold worth fourteen lakh rupees, it also had precious gems and jewels. The eight chiefs were given one lakh rupees each, elephants, horses, clothes and ornaments. Gaga Bhatt was given unlimited wealth. But Sir Yadunath Sarkar does not approve this description. According to him a maximum of fifty lakh rupees would have been spent.

Sanskrit Names to Administrative Posts

Affected by the Muslim rulers all the administration posts had either Persian names or Arabic names. Shivaji declared Marathi as his court language. '*Raj byawhar kosh*' (state terminology) was created for state affairs which was composed by several scholars under the direction of Raghunath Pant Hanumante. Though Shivaji had worn the title of *Chhatrapati* when he had declared his first independence, but now he did it in accordance with rules and regulation.

According to the new state terminology the eight chiefs of Shivaji were given the following names:

	Old name	**New name**
1.	Peshwa	— *Mukhya Pradhan (Pradhan Mantri)*
2.	Mazumdar	— *Amatya (Rajaswa Mantri)*
3.	Surnis	— *Sachiv (Vitt Mantri)*
4.	Wakenawees	— *Sachiv (Griha Mantri)*
5.	Sarnauwat	— *Senapati*
6.	Dabir	— *Sumant (Videsh Mantri)*
7.	Nyayadhish	— *Nyayadhish*
8.	Pandit Rao	— *Minister of religious affairs*

The first four of the above sat to the right side of the throne and the last four sat on the left.

Again a Mini Coronation

Mata Jijabai died only twelve days after the coronation on the 17th June 1674 in Pachar which was below Rajgarh. She was eighty then. Though it was not a matter to mourn because she had seen those glorious days which only rare mothers could see in their life time, but only after a few days of the coronation a *tantrik* named Nishchalpuri Gorabi came to Shivaji and said that his coronation could not prove good to him as 5th June was not an auspicious day according to the stars. Jijabai and one of his queens had died just after the coronation. He claimed the coronation itself was the only reason for these two deaths. He advised him to observe another coronation on some auspicious day. Shivaji did not see any loss in doing so.

A small coronation ceremony was held on the 24th of September 1674.

One Year after Coronation

The first year after coronation was a year of ups and downs for Shivaji. On the one hand he had had a few big successes but on the other hand he had to suffer a few blows also. A huge amount had been spent on the coronation which had emptied his treasury. To make that up he sent one of his troops to rob the Mughal province. The Mughal governor, Bahadur Khan, got this information well in advance. He proceeded to protect the village which was to be looted. In the meantime the Marathas attacked the main camp of the Mughal army and robbed it. They got one crore rupees and two hundred horses of a fine breed from there. After the loot they set the camp on fire and went away. Some more Mughal ruled provinces were looted after this. The Maratha blew up the city of Kalyan which was under the Mughals in Feb 1675.

When Shivaji was busy with his coronation ceremony, he had got the news that Bahadur Khan was preparing for a battle against him. So, in order to divert his attention, Shivaji sent a messenger to him with peace proposal during the rains, and this incidents of loot occurred. But still Bahadur Khan was finding himself unable to fight Shivaji so the compromise talks were continuing. In fact Shivaji wanted to take full advantage of the situation. Shivaji continued to talk about going into subordination of the Mughal empire from March to May 1675. Shivaji agreed to surrender seventeen of his forts to Mughals and to send his son Sambhaji in the service of the Mughal empire in the south as a six-thousand-strong *Mansabdar*. Bahadur Khan sent this proposal to Aurangzeb who also gave his consent. In the meantime before completion of the talk Shivaji returned Bahadur Khan's messenger after humiliating him and planned to capture Ponda, Karwar and Sondha in the beginning of May 1675. Shivaji blamed that Bahadur Khan had taken a huge amount from him in the name of the emperor.

From these failures of Bahadur Khan Aurangzeb made out that he was unable to suppress Shivaji. Bahadur Khan could not achieve even a single goal he had assured of. Shivaji had become a big challenge for Aurangzeb so he decided to send some other commander to south.

Purification of Netaji Palkar

Aurangzeb consulted Diler Khan on this topic. They both came on the conclusion that only such a person should be sent to suppress Shivaji who was well acquainted with the geography of south and was known to important local persons. Only one such person was there—Netaji Palkar. Now he was Md Kuli Khan as Aurangzeb had converted him into a Muslim. This proposal was sent to Md Kuli Khan and he agreed. He said, "I shall try my level best if I am given sufficient fund and arms and ammunition." Aurangzeb accepted all his demands. Md. Kuli Khan and Diler Khan started for the purpose. They gathered information about Shivaji's activities and camped near Satara.

Netaji Palkar was forcibly converted into a Muslim. Pobably he was very anxious for his salvation. So, one day, very early in the morning he fled away from the Mughal camp and met Shivaji. He told Shivaji all that had happened with him and also about the present plans of the Mughal. He had been in the north for eight years and his new family was still there. He requested Shivaji to convert him into a Hindu. So, after proper repentance and inspiration from Shivaji he was converted into a Hindu on 19th June 1676. He again came into the service of Shivaji and all of Aurangzeb's plan failed.

This incident tells about one special feature of Shivaji's character that he was not only a great conquerer, but also a great social reformer. This was a resounding slap on the faces of those orthodox Hindus who were not ready to accept anybody into their religion who followed any other religion. Other than Netaji Palkar, Shivaji had also reconverted Bajaji Nimbalkar from Muslim to Hindu on the inspiration of Mata Jijabai.

Control over the States under Bijapur

The strength of Bijapur was getting weaker day by day. Sultan Sikandar Adilshah was still only a child. The administration was in the hands of *wazir* Khawas Khan in reality. To take advantage of this situation Aurangzeb ordered Bahadur Khan and Dilar Khan to attack Bijapur. Probably Khawas Khan himself wanted to become the Sultan of Bijapur. He himself met Bahadur Khan at the bank of the Bhima river on 19th October 1675. Knowing about the conspiracy of Khawas Khan, the Afghan *sardar* of Bijapur, Bahlol Khan, arrested him in Bankipur on the 19th November and himself took charge of the estate.

In the meantime, the Portuguese colony in Goa were also looking carefully for their security. This carefulness of theirs joined by Bijapur was proving harmful for Shivaji. Shivaji's enemies could get arms and ammunitions from these coastal provinces. He wanted to develop his navy first to snatch away both trade and rule from the Europeans. Shivaji absorbed a politician, Pitambar Senoy, in his service because he was well acquainted with the problems and conflicts of the Europeans as he had worked as an interpreter to a British. Through Senoy, Shivaji got some good naval officers from Goa. Shivaji made a ship factory and an armoury in Malwan to utilize their services. The region between Kolaba and Malwan was already under Shivaji, but post of Goa in between was under the Portuguese, which was an obstacle for his naval force. Two very appropriate provinces Ponda and Karwar to the south of Goa were under Bijapur. It was necessary for him to capture these two in order to control the Portuguese and the Siddis of Janjira. Shivaji had tried to capture these two in August 1674, but could not succeed. Hence, Shivaji sent forty ships full of arms and ammunitions from Rajapur to conquer Ponda. Shivaji himself reached there on the 8th of April and surrounded Ponda. Bahlol Khan himself started with an army to protect Ponda but he was stopped on the way by one other Maratha army. The custodian of Ponda, Muhammad Khan, surrendered finding himself unable to protect it. Thus Ponda came under Shivaji with ease. Shivaji put a huge army to guard Ponda. Within a few days he also conquered the neighbouring provinces of Sondha and Karwar. Dharmaji Nagnath was appointed to manage these states.

Shivaji got these victories when his compromise talks with Bahadur Khan was going on.

Control over Vednoor

When Shivaji was in these newly conquered states, there was a queen ruling Vednoor, a small neighbouring state. Her commander had revolted. She requested Shivaji to suppress this revolt. Shivaji put the condition of *chouth* which was accepted so Shivaji helped her and suppressed the rebellion. Thus Shivaji got the right of getting *chouth* from Vednoor. He appointed Umaji Pandit as his representative for the *chouth* collection. He returned to Rajgarh via Rajapur on the 12th of June.

The Satara Fort was under the control of Bijapur. Shivaji captured this fort also on 11th November 1675. Shivaji liked this place very much so he stayed there for a few days. He dedicated the nearby port of Parli to his spiritual teacher Ramdas. Thus within a year of his coronation he conquered the whole of the western part of Bijapur.

Illness of Shivaji and Imprisonment of Sambhaji

In the end of 1675, when Shivaji was living in Satara, he fell seriously ill. Even a rumour of his death spread out. His son, Sambhaji, started adopting such habits which were just opposite to what Shivaji had hoped from him. So, in order to check his habits, he was kept in prison in Shringarpur the same year. Umaji Pandit was made responsible for his upkeep. After this he was kept under Samarth Ramdas but he showed no improvement. Probably this was the shock that had made Shivaji ill.

He fully recovered from this illness very soon probably in the beginning of 1676. After this Shivaji put stress on spreading his empire in south only.

Eight

Extension in the South

After the coronation Shivaji had acquired a state 200 miles in length and far less than this in width. Even he did not have control over the whole of the Maratha land. His authorized state was also surrounded by enemies from all sides. The vast Mughal empire was to its north, Bijapur in the east and Golkunda in the south. The Portuguese and the Siddi on the western coast could be harmful if they joined any of the enemies. He decided to extend his empire in south because north was blocked by the huge army arrangement of Mughals.

The region between the Krishna and Tungbhadra in south was under Bijapur. The administration here was controlled from the fort of Kopbal. Two Afghans, Hussain Khan Miyana and Abdur Rahim Khan, were the custodians of this fort. It was called the gateway of the south. Hindus of this region requested Shivaji to protect them from the atrocities of the Afghans. Even before this the ruler of Golkunda had invited Shivaji for compromise. Shivaji thought it better to punish the two Afghans while on way to Golkunda. Two armies under the leadership of Hummi Rao Mohite and Dhanaji Jadhav were sent for this purpose. These armies attacked Kopbal. The Marathas were victorious after a fierce fight. Abdul Rahim Khan was killed and Hussain Khan was arrested. Thus this area of Bijapur came under Shivaji's control.

Agreement with Golkunda

The year of 1672 proved to be very unlucky for both Golkunda and Bijapur as both lost their rulers in that year and fell in troubles. Abdullah Qutubshah had no son so the elder son-in-law, Syed Ahmad, tried to become the king but the commander-in-chief helped the younger son-in-law, Abul

Hassan. Resultantly Abul Hassan became the Sultan but the actual administration was grabbed by the commander-in-chief Syed Muzaffar, but Syed Muzaffar proved to be a tyrannical ruler. So Abdul Hassan expelled him from the rule with the help of Madan Pant and became full-fledged Sultan. Madan Pant was made the prime minister and was given the title of 'Surya Prakash'. As a result two groups were formed in the country—Hindu and Muslim. Madan Pant very skilfully worked on this post for ten years.

Shivaji's stepbrother Ekoji had established his state in South. He had a difference of opinion with his minister Raghunath Pant. He resigned from his service. Later he came in contact with Madan Pant. Both of them began dreaming of the glorious future of Hindus. Golkunda was in doldrums, so they convinced the Shah of Golkunda for a compromise with Shivaji. They made him meet Shivaji.

Messengers were sent from both the sides during this talk. At first the Shah of Golkunda expressed fear quoting the incidents of Afzal Khan and Shaista Khan. The messenger of Shivaji, Prahlad Niraji took the oath of his religion and assured him that Shivaji won't deceive him. Madan Pant also supported Nirajis statement. Finally Shah agreed.

Shivaji-Qutubshah Meeting

At first Shivaji also hesitated in meeting the Shah, but he prepared himself in 1676. While leaving for Golkunda he propagated that he was going to his stepbrother to discuss about the paternal property. Shivaji took his trustworthy *samants*—Netaji Palkar, Hammir Rao Mohit, Yesaji Kank, Anand Rao Makaji, Majaji More, Suryaji Malsure, Nila Prabhu Parasnis, Duttaji Wakenaurish and Balaji Aabji—alongwith an army of five thousand soldiers and set out for Golkunda. Perhaps he had taken the blessings of the Muslim *faqueer* Baba Yakub who lived in Kelsi near Dipoli and Mauni Baba of Bigula before going. He had given strict instruction to the soldiers not to touch the property of anybody in Golkunda and also not to misbehave with any woman. Hence, the five thousand soldiers remained disciplined.

The Shah of Golkunda wanted himself to go and welcome Shivaji, but Shivaji very politely sent a message: "You are elder so it is not justified for you to come so long to welcome me." So, Madan Pant, his brother Akatna and some senior *samants* went ten to twelve miles ahead of the city to welcome Shivaji and escorted him to the capital. The capital city was decorated like a newly wed bride. The roads were coloured with *Kumkum Kesar*. Lakhs of citizens in beautiful clothes and ornaments were standing to have a look of the brave Shivaji.

The soldiers of Shivaji had also put on special clothes. Embrodiered clothes were prepared for some special soldiers. Strings of pearls were hanging from their turbans and their hands had gold bangles. All the people were very eager to have a glimpse of the brave, cheerful, slim bodied Shivaji who was surrounded by commanders, ministers and bodyguards. People were applauding him. Women were showering flowers on him. He was adored with kindled lamps at many places. Shivaji presented clothes and ornaments to all the chiefs of every locality. Gold coins were squandered among the people.

In the end Shivaji reached the Dad Mahal of Qutub Shah. All stood peacefully. Only Shivaji alongwith five of his chief officers went into the court. The Shah came upto the gate to welcome him. They embraced each other. The Shah held him by hands and made him sit by his side. The minister, Madan Pant, sat on the ground and others kept standing. The *begums* of Shah were peeping through the nets of the *harem* with curiosity. This talk continued for three hours. The Shah listened to the wonderful incidents of Shivaji's life from his mouth. Then the Shah himself gave betel leaf and *itar* to Shivaji and clothes, elephants, horses to his ministers. When Shivaji got up to move, Shah escorted him to the gates of the Dad Mahal.

Structure of the Agreement

After all this the structure of the agreement was prepared. Followings were the conditions of the agreement:

1. The Shah of Golkunda will give Rs fifteen thousand per day to Shivaji and five thousand soldiers under his commander with all arms and ammunitions will help Shivaji in conquering Karnataka.

2. After Karnataka is conquered all the proviences, except that one which was under Shivaji's father Shahji, will be

given to the Shah of Golkunda.

3. Shivaji will at once reach for Shah's help in case the Mughals attack Golkunda.

4. Golkunda will pay Shivaji Rs. five lakh per year as tax.

This agreement was made secretly. The Shah gave Shivaji many a gift. His horse was decorated with pearl necklaces and gem necklaces. An interesting incident of this meeting is worth mentioning. One day Qutub Shah asked Shivaji, "How many elephants do you have?" Shivaji pointing towards his soldiers said, "These are my elephants." So there was a fight between Yesaji Kank and a strong elephant of Qutub Shah. Yesaji faced that elephant and cut off his trunk. The elephant ran away out of fear.

Worshipping Shree Shail

At the end of March 1677 Shivaji started from Golkunda, went to south and had a dip in the 'Nibriti Sangam'. From there he sent his army to Anantpur and went to Shree Shail alongwith a few bodyguards. This place is on a flat land at an altitude of one thousand feet from the Krishna river which is at a distance of seventy miles from Kurnul in the east. There is one of the twelve *Jyotilings* of Lord Shiva in Shree Shail, which is known as Mallikarjun. Shivaji worshipped here and gave away alms.

There is a temple of goddess Durga here. It is said that Shivaji had become ready to offer his head to the goddess. He drew his sword but goddess Durga appeared and stopped him. She said, "My child, you won't get salvation by this deed. Don't do so. You have yet to do many a work." Saying so she dispappeared.

Shivaji found this place very charming. So, he stayed there from 24th March to 1st April.

Capturing Jinji

Shivaji reached Madras from Shree Shail via Nandlal, Kadappa, Tirupati and Kalhasti. After worshipping in the Tirupati temple he sent his army of five thousand soldiers to capture Jinji. The army surrounded the fort. Custodian of the fort, Nasir Muhammad Khan, was given some money and was assured of a *Jagir* earning Rs fifty thousand yearly. Hence, he handed over the fort to Marathas on 13th May. On hearing this Shivaji at once reached Jinji. The old wall was demolished and a new and strong wall was built around the fort. Raiji Nagle was made the new custodian of the fort and Bitthal Pildeo Atre the new revenue manager of the area. Jinji was made the centre of administration in Karnataka.

Control over Vellore and Valigandapuram

After capturing Jinji Shivaji set out for Vellore on 23rd May. This fort was invincible like Jinji. It was under an officer of Bijapur, Habshi Abdullah Khan. The Maratha army surrounded Villore Fort. It was not easy to conquer this fort. Shivaji's army captured two neighbouring hills. The battle continued for fourteen months. Only one hundred out of five hundred soldiers were remaining in the fort. Abdullah khan was sure that he was not going to get any help from outside. So when he got an offer of Rs one and a half lakh and a Jagir of the same annual income, he surrendered the fort to Marathas either in July or August 1676.

A pathan *samant* of Bijapur, Sher Khan Lodhi had captured a large land area. He himself lived in Valigandapuram near Trichanapalli. Sher Khan Lodhi was an incompetent ruler and ruled his territory with the help of his Brahmin ministers. His ministers had assured him that Shivaji could not harm him in any way whereas his friend, the ruler of Pondicherry Francioya Martin had warned him that he should always be careful from Shivaji.

When Marathas had surrounded Vellore, Shivaji had assessed that the business would take a long time so he set out to conquer Sher Khan Lodhi. Sher Khan alongwith all his army faced Shivaji near Tiruwari. Sher Khan fled from the battle out of fear. He hid in the fort of Tiruwari. From there he ran away to Kaddalore at night and from Kaddalore he took 100 soldiers with him and went to the small fort of Bhuwangiri Pattan, twenty two miles away from there. Marathas snatched away his five hundred horses, two elephants and twenty camels. This way Shivaji captured many of his cities and forts. Finally helpless Sher Khan surrendered on 5th July 1677. Thus the coastal area of Karnataka from Tungabhadra to Kaveri came under Shivaji.

It is notable that according to the agreement with Golkunda, Jinji was to be handed over to Golkunda, but

Shivaji did not do so, and as a result Golkunda stopped paying Rs fifteen thousand daily to Shivaji. Then Shivaji prepared a list of the property of all the wealthy people of the state. He wrote letters to the richest men and demanded a loan of Rs ten lakh. In fact, this was not a loan, but it was *chouth*. Who would dare to ask it back from Shivaji?

Conflict over Paternal Property and the Solution

Shahji had two legal wives—Jijabai and Tukabai. Jijabai has two sons—Sambhaji and Shivaji. Tukabai gave birth to one son, Ekoji. Ekoji and Sambhaji were sent to suppress a rebal *sardar* in 1654 where Sambhaji was killed. So, now Shahji had only two sons—Shivaji and Ekoji.

Dadaji Konddeo and Naropant Trimul Hanumante were Shahji's two most trustworthy servants. Shahji had sent Dadoji Konddeo to upkeep Shivaji. After the death of Naropant, Shahji sent his elder son Janardan Pant to Shivaji and younger, Raghunath Pant, remained in Karnataka in the service of Shahji. Ekoji had almost caputed Tanjaur, a province of Bijapur. He also performed his coronation ceremony on 17th March, 1675. Immediately after this there was a conflict between Ekoji and Raghunath Pant. Raghunath Pant asked Ekoji his permission to go to Kashi. He was permitted but instead of going to Kashi he went to Bijapur. Later he came in contact with Madan Pant, the minister of Golkunda. This episode has already been mentioned earlier.

After humiliating Sher Khan Shivaji decided to meet his stepbrother, Ekoji. He marched towards Tanjaur and camped in Tirumwari, ten miles to the north of Tanjaur. He demanded Rs one crore as tax from the ruler of Madura. Finally it was fixed Rs thirty lakh. When Shivaji got the money he promised not to attack Madura.

Ekoji came to meet his elder brother in his camp. Peshwa Jagannath Pant and some soldiers were with him. Ekoji had fought many battles against Shivaji in favour of Bijapur, but Shivaji did not talk of that. Both of them had many talks either in loneliness or before everybody, took meals together. Ekoji neither supported nor opposed Shivaji's words. He never expressed whatever he had in his mind. Shahji was in Bangalore at the time of his death so, all his property and the territory of Karnatakan had come under Ekoji. Shivaji had written earlier also demanding his share in this property and Ekoji had only replied, "Your orders are greatly acceptable."

Here also Shivaji demanded his share. Being the elder of the two, Shivaji wanted only three-fourth of the total, but Ekoji refused to give. At this Shivaji became angry. He threatened Ekoji. Pressure was mounting on Ekoji. So, one night he fled away crossing the Kolerun river because he knew Shivaji won't leave him until he obeys him. He fled away to Tanjaur. People who had come with him were arrested. This happened in July, 1677.

Shivaji was in fact very unhappy when he got the news of Ekojis escape. He spoke, "Why did he escape! If he did not want to give what I had asked for, he would have told me and I would have left everything for him. But young boy is a young boy only. He finally showed his childishness." The people who had been arrested were sent giving rewards.

After this Shivaji sent three of his men to Ekoji. He also wrote a letter in which he wrote clearly that Ekoji had to give his share in the paternal property. Now Ekoji showed his true colour. He wrote denying very clearly Shivaji's share in the paternal property, "Whatever our father has gained, it was from the service of Bijapur for whom Shivaji Raje had always been an enemy and a traitor. His activity has shocked our father. There is no paternal property other than that earned through the service of Bijapur. I am a loyal servant of Bijapur and hence I am bound to its order."

It was clear that in spite of having goodwill Ekoji was ready to fight against Shivaji. He asked Madura and Mysore for help against Shivaji and informed about all that had happened between him and Shivaji, but there was no reaction from Bijapur.

Shivaji had been out of his home state for last ten months. He also got the information that the Mughal governor, joining hands with Bijapur, had attacked Golkunda. Shivaji had friendship with Golkunda. So, Shivaji decided to return to his state. He left Bahir Rao Mohite, Hambir Rao and Raghunath Pant along with a big army in south so that they could manage compromise with Ekoji and himself returned to Maharashtra from the coast of Kolerun on 27th July. On the way he captured Arni, Kolar, Hoskote, Bangalore, Balapur and Shira districts—a large land portion to the north of Kaveri river which was earlier under Ekoji. He appointed his new officer to rule there.

When he reached Gadag on his way back, he got the news of Ekoji's attack. Ekoji attacked Valigandapuram with fourteen thousand soldiers on 16th November 1677. Shivaji's army was defeated after a day's battle. At night Shivaji's army suddenly attacked Ekoji's army when they were taking rest. Ekoji's army could not counter the attack. Some of the officers were arrested and the rest of the army fled away to Tanjaur. When Shivaji got this news he wrote a letter to his brother on 1st March, 1678, "Gods are kind to me. I have been able to defeat the Turks with their blessings. How can you hope of defeating me with the help of those Turks? You should not oppose my army directly. Whatever has happened can't be mended. Take lesson from that and give up your obstinacy. You have kept all our father's property forcibly for thirteen years and now I have taken my share. Please hand over Arni, Bangalore, Kolar, Hoskote, Shiral Kot and Tanjaur to my officers. Give me half of the cash, ornaments, horses, elephants and other property and compromise with me. I shall give a *jagir* earning three lakh hones yearly between Tungbhadra and Panhala. Or if you don't want to take this from me as a gift, I shall request Qutub Shah to give you an equal *jagir* in his state. Thus you have two options, accept whatever you wish: Give up your obstinacy and put an end to our family conflict. If you accept my proposal, you will always be happy. If not, you yourself will increase your troubles and then I won't be able to protect you."

Ekoji could not be pacified even by this letter. He could not decide what he should do. His wife Dipabai acted very wisely at such an hour. She convinced her husband that it was good to go according to Shivaji. Dipabai expelled all his Muslim advisors and requested him to call their ex-minister, Raghunath. Ekoji called Raghunath. These two found out the solution to the conflict of paternal property. All that description was sent to Shivaji who became very happy. He praised the role of Dipabai.

There were total nineteen sections of this agreement. Out of those the 6th, 12th, 15th, 16th, 17th and 19th were very important. They were as follows:

The 6th did not allow any anti-Hindu or wicked person to live in the state. It was written in the 12th: "When there was a peace pact between me and Adil Shah in the mediatorship of our father, it was clearly mentioned there that neither of us would go into the service of Bijapur. We would help them as well-wishers, and not as servants, if required. We will have to follow this pact in future. So Ekoji should take himself as a servant of Bijapur."

15th: "I have already captured Bangalore, Hoskote, and Shira. I willingly give it to my brother's wife Dipabai. At the death of Dipabai it can be given to her daughter or whomever she wants."

16th: "I have conquered Tanjaur and the neighbouring districts. I give them back to Ekoji who will be their sole owner."

17th: "I give a province earning one lakh to Raghunath. This will always remain with him or his descendants."

19th: "Ekoji will maintain our father's grave."

This agreement put an end to the conflict between the two brothers, but Ekoji was very sad for losing his independence. The officers, sent by Shivaji, captured all his property. They did not even consult him in the administrative matters. This upset Ekoji and he gave up all amusements. At this Shivaji wrote a letter of consolation to him. Unfortunately Shivaji died within three months.

Nine

Evening Time

The Maratha empire had become a well organised state with the inclusion of many of the Karnataka provinces. Sufficient efforts were made to secure this. Many enthusiastic Maratha youth were properly trained for its stability only. Hammir Rao, Janardan Pant, Santaji Bhosle, Santaji Ghorpare, Dhanaji Jadhav etc got the knowledge of politics during the Karantaka campaign only. They set up good management in Karanataka with their skill. The *jagirdars*, *samants* and people of Karantaka were fully satisfied with the policies of the Maratha administration. Hence, they accepted the rule of Shivaji by heart.

Shivaji returned to Maharashtra from the Karantaka campaign. He robbed the Kanara Balghat regions on the return journey. He reached a place named Belbari, about thirty miles to the south of the Bedgaon Fort in this consequence. The *zamindars* here snatched away some of his things. Shivaji surrounded the Fort of Belbari. This fort was owned by the widow of the ex-*jagirdar*, Savitribai. This lady countered the victorious Shivaji for twenty seven days. But lastly she had to surrender as food and the arms and ammunitions could not reach her. As a result Belbari came under Shivaji.

Revolt of Sambhaji

Sambhaji was the eldest son of Shivaji. Shivaji had declared him the prince on the occasion of his coronation. He was born on 14th May 1657. His mother, Sai Bai, died only two years after his birth. He had gone to Agra alongwith his father when he was only nine, where they both were imprisoned and due to Shivaji's wisdom they were able to escape. After that he worked as a *mansabdar* in the Mughal army in Aurangabad where he was spoiled. Though he was very handsome to look at, sportive, skilled in warfare and well-qualified, but the company of the Mughal brought many evils in his character.

Sambhaji was centre of his father's hopes. Shivaji had arranged proper education for him. Teachers like Keshav Bhatt Purohit and Kavi Kalash were kept for him. He was also given the knowledge of politics. But he had washed away all the hopes of Shivaji. He had started getting the information of Sambhaji's ill-character after his coronation only. They say that Sambhaji had infringed the modesty of a Brahmin woman. When Shivaji returned to Maharashtra after Karnataka triumph he found that Sambhaji had adopted more bad habits so once again he had to imprison him. He was kept in the Panhala Fort.

Shviaji's enemies were very happy to see his son going on the wrong path. The Mughal commander, Diler Khan, got the news of Sambhaji's imprisonment through his spies. He found it an appropriate chance and started to spread his net. He sent his spies to lure Sambhaji. Sambhaji was unhappy due to the hard behaviour of his father so he was caught in Diler Khan's net. He somehow escaped with his wife Yesubai in the night of 13th December, 1678. He reached Bahadurgarh where Diler Khan had camped his army. Diler Khan was waiting for this moment only. He showed love and affection to Sambhaji. He was very glad at this success. He sent all this information to Aurangzeb. He also became very happy. He offered Sambhaji seven-thousand-strong *Mansabdars* and an elephant. Apparently Sambhaji got all this but Aurangzeb cautioned Diler Khan that it might be a trick of Shivaji, so he should be careful.

After this Sambhaji and Diler Khan planned to conquer Bijapur and set out with a large aremy. They first attacked Bhupalgarh on the way. This fort was under the Marathas. Firangoji Narsal was the custodian here. There was a huge treasure in this fort. Sambhaji told Diler Khan about the treasure. Firangoji could counter with cannons but it might have killed Sambhaji so he could not do so. As a result Diler Khan captured Bhupalgarh on 2nd April 1679. This news gave Shivaji a big shock. He scolded Firangoji and asked him why he did not kill a sinner like Sambhaji. Diler Khan and Sambhaji proceeded towards Bijapur.

The Bijapur state was in a miserable condition that time. *Wazir* Bahlol Khan died on 23rd December 1677. After him one of his slaves, Jamshed Khan, became the custodian of the minor Sultan Sikandar Adil Shah. He was the custodian of the fort also, but he was an incompetent and timid person. Shivaji found it a good time to conquer Bijapur so he lured Jamshed Khan and wanted to turn him in his favour. He became ready to hand over the fort as well as the child Sultan in return of Rs thirty lakhs. Siddi Masood got this information. He played a trick. He propagated that he had fallen ill. Some days later people heard that he had died. His four thousand soldiers went to Jamshed Khan and requested him to keep them in his service. They were employed in the fort. These soldiers arrested Jamshed Khan and opened the gates of the fort. Siddi Massood became the *wazir* of Bijapur on 21st February, 1678. Shivaji's plan could not succeed.

When Diler Khan and Sambhaji marched to conquer Bijapur, Siddi Massood requested Shivaji to help. He wrote in his letter, "You have also eaten the salt of the Adil Shah family and we both are the residents of the same country. The Mughals are our enemies. It will be better if we both join hands to defeat them."

Shivaji accepted this request and set out for Bijapur with a large army. By then Diler Khan had surrounded Bijapur. He was trying to capture Bijapur with force. Shivaji organised the battle skilfully. The enclosure remained for two months. In the end Diler Khan had to lift the siege being helpless. Siddi Masood expressed his gratitude to Shivaji for this help. Then there was an agreement between Bijapur and Shivaji. According to this agreement Bijapur approved of Shivaji's control over Tanjaur, Jinji and Kopbal. After this he sent Shivaji giving him many gifts.

Return of Sambhaji

After returning from Bijapur Diler Khan planned to conquer Panhala. He set out for Panhala with Sambhaji. He tortured Marathas on the way. Many rich people in Tikota begged for mercy but he robbed everything of theirs who had come in his shelter. He did not spare even Muslims. Many a people committed suicide by jumping into the wells to avoid insult. Thousands of people were arrested and asked for ransom. He also robbed Athani. He oppressed the Hindus severly. People begged for mercy form Sambhaji in the name of his father. Sambhaji was touched. He was never in favour of such atrocity. He adivsed Diler Khan not to do so, but Diler Khan told Sambhaji very clearly that he would do whatever he wished. He did not require any advice. He said, "I am the master of myself. You need not preach me good conducts."

Sambhaji was much ashamed of himself getting such a reply. He revolted against his father and ran away. He understood that his friendship with Diler Khan won't last long. He thought that life in his father's prison was better than being insulted. And Aurangzeb was also unhappy with him due to the failure of the Bijapur campaign.

Shivaji was also worried about his son. He had asked his spies to try to get him freed from the Mughal clutches because he had pick up bad habits in the company of the Mughal and now again he had gone into their company. Aurangzeb was in a pensive mood due to the defeat of his army in Bijapur. So he called Diler Khan back and deputed Bahadur Khan in his place. He sent a strict order to Diler Khan to arrest Sambhaji. Sambhaji was quite unaware of this conspiracy. Mahadji Nimbalkar, a Maratha, a *samant* under Diler Khan, was also in the Mughal army then. He was husband of Sambhaji's sister Sakwarbai. He told Sambhaji about the above conspiracy. Sambhaji realized that inborn enemies could never become friends. So, he started thinking to get rid of the Mughals.

Sambhaji took his wife in the disguise of a man and in the night of 20th November 1679 escaped from the Athani Mughal camp. That time he had only ten bodyguards with him. He reached Bijapur from Athani and asked Masood Khan for shelter. Diler Khan got the information of Sambhaji reaching Bijapur. So he sent a proposal to Masood Khan that he would get Rs thirty lakhs if he handed over Sambhaji to Mughals. Sambhaji also got all this information. So, he left Bijapur in the night of 30th November.

Shivaji had formed a special army troop to watch Sambhaji. Sambhaji came in contact with this troop and finally reached Panhala on 14th December.

Loot in Jalnapur

When Shivaji was fighting Diler Khan in order to help

Bijapur, he thought of a trick to divert Diler Khan's attention. He divided his army into two parts. He kept one part with him and sent the other part under the leadership of Anandrao Makaji. This army led by Shivaji entered the Mughal territory through Sailgur on 4th November. Robbing the people this army reached Jalana, forty miles to the east of Aurangabad on 15th November. Jalana was a centre of trade and a rich city. They robbed the people upto their satisfaction, but they did not get much wealth as they had hoped. It was later known that all the rich people taking their wealth had fled away to the shrine of a Muslim *faqir* Syed Jaan Muhammad because they knew that Shivaji respected all religions, hence they were safe there. But it did not happen so. The Maratha soldiers entered the shrine and robbed all that they got there. The *faqir* of the shrine tried to stop them but they did not listen to him and also abused him. At this the *faqir* cursed Shivaji. It is said that Shivaji died only after five months of this incident.

The Maratha returned after robbing Jalnapur. Suddenly, a large Mughal army attacked them near Sangamner under the leadership of Ranmast Khan. Sidhoji Nimbalkar and Santaji Ghorpare countered them. This battle continued for three days. Sidhoji Nimbalkar and two thousand Maratha soldiers died in this battle. A large Mughal army had started from Aurangabad to take part in this battle. On the third night of the battle this new army camped six miles away from the battlefield. Shivaji was surrounded from all sides. There was no scope of an escape. Meanwhile the commander of the new army, Keshari Singh, sent a secret message to Shivaji to run away leaving everything before the front path was blocked. Seeing the seriousness of the situation Shivaji took only 500 solders with him and ran away. He reached the Pattagarh Fort. Four thousand soldiers were killed, many alongwith Hambir Rao were injured and many were arrested by the Mughal army in this battle. After this Shivaji took rest in Pattagarh Fort so it was renamed Vishramgarh.

A Letter to Aurangzeb Opposing *Jajiya*

Aurangzeb issued an order on 3rd April, 1679 to count all the Hindus in the Mughal territories and collect *Jajiya* tax from them. This tax was to be collected from all the Hindus on the basis of their income. The tax was classified into three categories according to income. It was fixed to collect 13 rupees 13 annas from high income group, 6 rupees 9 annas from middle income group and 3 rupees 5 annas from low income group.

The collection of this tax had been stopped for many years, but Aurangzeb had re-started it showing his hatred for Hindus. Shivaji wrote a letter to Aurangzeb protesting this. The letter read as follows:

Badshah Alamgir,

Salam!

I, Shivaji, am a well-wisher of yours. Thanking for your grand kindness I request you that though I was compelled to give up your glorious company without seeking permission from you, I am always ready to carry out my duties as your servant.

I have heard that your royal treasury has been emptied due to the battles against me and so you have ordered to collect *Jajiya* tax form the Hindus to make up for that.

Your Majesty! Akbar ruled for 52 years. He had adopted a very good policy of keeping friendly relations with all the religious sects. Protection and nourishment of all was the only goal of his noble heart. He was called '*Jagat Guru*' only for this reason.

After him Badshah Jehangir bestowed his kindness upon the world for 22 years. He devoted all his life to public welfare. Badshah Shahjahan also ruled for 32 years and got a good name.

There was such a good effect of Akbar's generosity that wherever he went, victory and success automatically came to him. One can easily understand the power and glory of the ancient emperors following whose politics your highness became restless and perplexed. They could also have imposed the *Jajiya* tax, but there was no room for superstition in their hearts because they knew that God has made high and low to show their belief in different religions and their different mentalities. Their kindness and generosity will always remain in the pages of history. Good luck or bad luck come due to the strong heartily desire of people. Their wealth kept on increasing day by day because people had praises and wishes for these emperors in their heart and all their works were successful.

And in your regime, most of the forts and territories have

slipped from your hand and the remaining will also have the same fate because I won't leave any stone unturned to destroy them. The people are crushed in your regime. The income of every village has decreased. Rs one thousand instead of one lakh and Rs ten in place of one thousand is collected and that also with great difficulty. The army is unstable in your empire. The Muslims cry and the Hindus burn. Often all the people could not get the evening meal.

How did your royal heart allow you to impose *Jajiya* tax in such a pitiable condition of the people? You will very soon be defamed from west to east that you are lured by the beggars' plates and that you collect *Jajiya* tax from Brahmin priests, the Jain monks, saints, bankrupts, poor and the victims of famine and also that your valour is exhibited in snatching the alms bags. You have destroyed the name of the Taimur family and your own respect.

Your Highness! If you have faith in the holy book, *Quran*, please look into it. It is written there that God is the master of all and not of only Muslims. In fact Hinduism and Islam are only two different words.

Azan is offered in the mosque to remember the Lord and in temple a large bell is rung. Hence to show orthodoxy for one's religion and rituals is nothing else but changing the thoughts of the holy books.

In fact *Jajiya* is no way justified according to the religion. If you look at it politically, it can be applicable there, where beautiful women wearing valuable ornaments are free to move from one place to the other without any hindrance. But now-adays when your big cities are looted, the imposition of Jajiya is quite illegal. Moreover, in India it is a new tyranny and completely harmful as well.

If you think that your religion will be recognized only by torturing the people and frightening the Hindus, first you collect *Jajiya* from the lord of the Hindus, Maharana Raj Singh. And then it won't be difficult to collect it from me as I am always committed to your service. There is no valour in troubling these little people.

I cannot understand why your officers are so loyal that they do not reveal the actual situation of the country before you, but want to hide the fire with pieces of straw.

May your empire spread splendour in the sky like the Sun!

Unsuccessful Efforts to Convince Sambhaji

As soon as Sambhaji reached Panhala, Shivaji tightened the security arrangement there because he thought Diler Khan might attack Panhala, but Diler Khan had also understood that it was not easy to conquer Panhala, so he did not dare do so.

Shivaji also reached Panhala and stayed there for two months. He made tireless efforts to bring Sambhaji on the right track. He was made to realize that the responsibilities of the great Maratha empire was to be shifted over to his shoulders in near future. He got the state's property statement prepared only to indicate that Sambhaji should follow the path of good character which would help him protect the state and its property. Sambhaji was not a child now. He had also gained political knowledge living in the company of Diler Khan. So it was not possible to force him to do anything. Shivaji used many different ways, but failed to convince Sambhaji.

Shivaji's Family Conflict and Illness

Shivaji got a big blow by Sambhaji's bad character. His first wife had died. There was scarcity of modesty, peace etc. good conducts in the character of Soyarabai, the mother of his second son, Rajaram. They say that she wanted to make her son the king. She put pressure on Shivaji for this again and again and never left a chance of conspiring for the purpose. When Sambhaji had fled away to Diler Khan she did not allow Shivaji to live peacefully even for a moment. As a result the family life of Chhatrapati Shivaji became quite disturbed. This disturbance affected the relationship between Shivaji and Sambhaji to a great extent. Hence, Sambhaji was again arrested and imprisoned in Panhala. He deputed Hiroji Furzand, Somji Nayak and Vitthal Trayambak for strict vigil on Sambhaji and went away to Sajjangarh.

Shivaji was quite disappointed of his son's bad character and disturbed family atmosphere. Resultantly his health started deteriorating very quickly. He went to the '*Ashram*' of Samarth Ramdas to meet him on 31st December 1679. He stayed there for three days and kept himself busy in worshipping and listening to the preachings of Samarth Ramdas. Samarth Ramdas understood that his end was fast approaching.

Shivaji returned to Rajgarh on 4th February. He had also realized that his end was near. He decided to perform the thread ceremony and marriage ceremony of his ten-year-old son Rajaram in order to carry out a father's duties. The thread ceremony was observed on 7th March 1680. He married to Pratap Rao Gujar's daughter, Janakibai, only one week later on the 15th of March.

End of Journey of Life

Shivaji had been sick those days. He had fever on 23rd March and then blood dysentery. Food and water intake had lessened. Now this fever and blood dysentery weakened his health more and more. He summoned his officers and delivered his last preaching, "The soul is immortal. We will come to the earth again and again." His throat was blocked and he could not speak further.

When it was sure that Shivaji was not going to survive, a proposal was sent to Sambhaji in Panhala that the state should be divided between the two brothers but he did not accept it. In the afternoon of 3rd April, 1680, Saturday, the near relations present there and the officers saw that Shivaji was about to breathe his last. The water of Ganges was put into his mouth and Chhatrapati Shivaji Maharaj breathed his last. The great conqueror Chhatrapati Shivaji slept for ever. Not only the whole Maratha kingdom, but each and every Hindu individual was filled with deep grief.

Shivaji's Wives and Offsprings

There is a difference of opinion among the historians regarding the number of wives and daughters of Shivaji. Dr. Yadunath Sarkar admits that Shivaji had five wives and three daughters whereas Sardesai claims that he had eight wives and six daughters but both of them accept that he had only two sons. The names of all his eight wives have been mentioned in the book. Here a brief introduction of his offsprings is being given.

Sons

Shivaji had two sons. The first was Sambhaji who was born on the 14th of May, 1657 from the womb of Saibai and the second was Rajaram born from Soyarabai on 14th February 1670.

Daughters

Saibai gave birth to three daughters—Sakwarbai, Ranubai and Ambikabai. The fourth daughter Nanabai was born from Sagunbai, Shivaji's second wife. The daughter born from Soyarabai was Balabai or Dipabai. The sixth daughter Kamaljabai was born from Shivaji's sixth wife Sakwarbai.

Dr. Yadunath Sarkar has mentioned only five names as Shivajis wives—Saibai, Soyarabai, Putlibai, Sakwarbai and Kashibai. And according to him Shivaji had only three daughters—Sakwarbai alias Sakhubai, Ambikabai and Nanabai alias Rajkunwarbai.

Only three wives of Shivaji was alive at the time of his death—Soyarabai, Putlibai and Sakwarbai. Putlibai performed *Sati* on Shivaji's funeral pyre.

The Spiritual Teachers of Chhatrapati Shivaji

The famous historian Govind Sakharam Sardesai has mentioned that Shivaji had relations with fourteen spiritual persons—Tukaram Baba, Samarth Ramdas, Mauni Baba, Nishchalpuri Gosavi, Paramanand Baba, Jairam Swami, Narayan Deo, Rangnath Swami, Bitthal Swami, Bhanudas Baba, Anandmurti, Bodhale Baba, Baba Yakut and Trayambak Narayan.

There was none among the descendants of Shivaji who could maintain the state established by him. Very soon the internal dispute of the Chhatrapati family was exposed. The coronation ceremony of Rajaram was held in Rajgarh in April 1680. Sambhaji imprisoned him in July and became Chhatrapati. He got Anaji Dutto and his brother Somaji murdered in 1681 and sentenced Soyarabai to death blaming her of poisoning Shivaji. He himself was caught by the Mughals after Shivaji's death and Aurangzeb killed him on 11th March 1681. With the passage of time the Peshawas captured the empire established by Chhatrapati Shivaji.

Ten

Appraisal of Shivaji

Not only in Indian history but in the international history also Shivaji's personality is uncomparable and extraordinary. His life was an ideal combination of many virtues like understanding, dutifulness, good character, communal harmony etc. A complete assessment of Shivaji's character and works can be a topic for research. Light is being thrown here on his virtues in brief:

A Great Epoch-Maker

Shivaji was the son of a simple *jagirdar*. He became the founder of the Maratha empire on his own strength. He added a new chapter in history and started a new age. First of all he unified the Mawals who were considered wild and uncultured by the society. After this he united simple farmers, local *jagirdars* under the Muslim rulers and *samants* of Maharashtra and established a state. Then in the end he defeated all the dynasties of South India with his strength. He did not lag behind in challenging the then Mughal emperor openly. Though the emperor and the then Muslim historians tried to prove him unimportant calling him a *bandit*, a hill rat and rustic etc but the time arrived and the critics accepted him as a great epoch-maker. It is also true that his minister Ram Chandra Neelkanth had made Shivaji's assessment in his life time only, but people could not know about it. Portions of Neelkanth's assessment are given below:

"The epoch-maker Shivaji was first dependent to a Muslim, but at the age of 15 years he started his work of making Poona his independent state. This small start became the base of his greatness. First he was surrounded by three kingdoms—Adilshahi, Qutubshahi and Nizamshahi and later he surrounded the three by his skill."

His great virtues attracted not only the Indian critics but also the foreigners. Sir Richard Tample wrote in his book Poorviya Anubhav, "Shivaji was not only a brave man, but had an extraordinary power with which he could inculcate zeal in others. He lifted a low community and carried it to the status of an empire." Apart from these Shivaji was a great administrator (ruler). Sir Yadunath Sarkar has said, "Shivaji was the last nation maker having an extraordinary knowledge of great making. He blew new life into the Maratha community. He proved with his own example that the Hindu community can make a nation and can establish a state. Shivaji made it clear that in fact the tree of Hinduism has not dried.

An Ideal Politician

Shivaji's successes are the proof of his being an ideal politican. Though he was not much educated, yet all the politicians of the world bowed down before him due to his superhuman political wisdom. There was no room for suicidal benediction in his politics. Possibly his custodians would have given the practical knowledge of politics. Praising Shivaji's political skill a western critic, Eckworth, has written, "To measure the power with which he worked by his victories will be an incomplete one. None of the people of his time had such minute and correct knowledge of the enemy's strength or weakness." The whole of Shivaji's life was full of struggles and efforts. For that it was necessary that he should make his plans successful so secretly that the minimum people could pay attention to it.

He had defeated all his enemies through his political wisdom. His contemporary philospher Barnier had written, "This man Shivaji is working with the complete personality of an independent king. He laughs at his condemnation by the Mughal emperor or the Sultan of Bijapur. He strikes again and again and robs all the territories from Surat to Goa. He draws attention of the Mughal emperor, Aurangzeb, by his courage and continuous labour and makes the Indian army so busy that the Mughal army doesn't get a chance to conquer Bijapur."

It was the greatest proof of his praiseworthy political wisdom that even his obdurate enemy, Aurangzeb, praised him. Aurangzeb said at Shivaji's death, "He was the only man who showed the importance of making new states wheras I have been trying to destroy the old states. He was a great commander. My armies kept on trying against him for nineteen years, nevertheless he continued to extend his empire."

In fact a nation and its development depends upon the ability of its ruler. If a nation suffers from lackings or mischiefs, it denotes the incapabitlity of its ruler. Shivaji is a good example of this.

Extraordinary Administrator

To run a government requires sharp administrative skill along with good political knowledge. After establishing an independent society Shivaji changed some traditional rules completely. His plan of eight chiefs was a part of this change. He himself was a *jagirdar*, but became an independent ruler by virtue of his own strength. Therefore he changed the practice of giving away *jagir* in spite of salary to servants, because these *jagirdars* only created problems for the state. Govind Sakharam Sardesai has quoted the main principles of his administration as:

1. Protection of the state through strong forts.
2. Cash salary for services.
3. Appointment on the basis of qualification and not heredity.
4. Collection of revenue by trustworthy people.
5. Eradication of giving land on contract.
6. Establishment of administrative departments.
7. Equal opportunity for all in services without discrimination of caste of creed.
8. To prpare the annual budget in such a way that there must be some profit.

An administrator must have character based virtues which Shivaji had in plenty. This was the secret of his success.

A Worshipper of the Indian Culture

Culture is the soul of a nation. Though the universal compliance seems to be impossible, but every nationalist must be proud of his culture. Hating culture is a symbol of destruction.

In fact the cultural inspiration was only active behind all the progress of Chhatrapati Shivaji. Conspiracy to destroy

Indian culture was on during the Muslim rule in India. Forcible conversion of religion, demolition of Hidnu temples and schools etc were the result of this conspiracy. How could an epoch-maker like Shivaji tolerate such insult to his culture?

Mother is called the super god in the Indian culture. It is clear from the study of Shivaji's biography that he respected his mother like a god in reality. Touching his mother's feet while going somewhere or starting some work was inseparable part of his life. He had great respect for saints without any discrimination. He had unique reverence for temples, mosques or churches etc. Govind Sakharam Sardesai writes:

"Goddesses, gods, Brahmins, saints, temples etc always remained in his heart. It is a historical fact that wherever Shivaji went, he first of all got information about the temples in the neighbouring area and the spiritual people coming there."

He always supported the bright aspects of culture but at the same time he was quite opposed to castewise narrowness, conventions etc. Due to his love for culture he got his coronation ceremony performed according to the ancient Indian culture and at the same time opposed the orthodox Brahmins in order to prove himself a 'Kshatriya'. He also revived the cultural aspect of caste system based on work.

Praiseworthy Virtues Related to Character

The importance of orders and preachings of a man goes according to his strength of character and the importance of character increases according to the post he holds. If the administrator has high character, his subjects don't have the courge of doing any anti-social or characterless work. Hence, you can hope of good character from the public only if the ruler has the best and praiseworthy character. Shivaji was well acquainted with this fact. Therefore one could easily locate his great virtue of character from his usual activities.

Abji Sondeo had arrested the beautiful daughter-in-law of the Muslim governor of Kalyan, Mulla Ahmad, and had sent her to Shivaji as a gift. Shivaji called her mother and with due respect sent her to her husband. This high character and self control was the top secret of his life. Even the Muslim philosophers have praised Shivaji. Khafi Khan, a critic, has written, "Shivaji always tried to protect the honour of his subjects. He always robbed the travellers and troubled the people, but he always kept himself away from shameful works, and when chances came, he protected the chastity of even Muslim women. He had given strict orders in this regard and whoever disobeyed was punished. The Muslim Sultans or commanders always kept prostitutes with them even during the battles but Shivaji was far away from this." The French ambassador Germain had met Shivaji in 1677 in his battle camp. He writes, "There was no pomp and show in Shivaji's camp. There were no women—only two tents made of rough cloth." Dr. Yadunath Sarkar has written, "Shivaji's character was full of virtues. His devotion to mothers, love for the offsprings, control over senses, labouriousness, liberty to all communities, attachment to religion and luxury avoidance was incomparable. He protected the chastity of women even if he had to apply all his strength."

Supporter of Communal Harmony

Though Shivaji aimed at establishing a Hindu State, he wanted renaissance of the degraded Hindu. Love for one's religion does not mean enmity with other communities. Akbar the great had been an open example of this. Shivaji never discriminated between man and man on the basis of religion or community. The main reason for his enmity with Aurangzeb was this only. He opposed Aurangzeb very strongly through a letter when the latter imposed *Jajiya* tax on Hindus.

Shivaji never showed hatred for Islam or any other religion while protecting his religion. He gave equal respect to Muslim *faqirs* as he gave to Hindu saints. There was no room for appointment on the basis of caste or religion in his state. The chief officer of his navy Daulat Khan and Siddi and the foreign minister Mulla Haidar all were Muslims. He had full faith on these officers. Mulla Haidar had once gone to the Mughal governor Bahadur Khan with a peace proposal as the representative of Shivaji. Comparing the love of both Aurangzeb and Shivaji for their religion Ekwarth writes, "Shivaji's character is much higher than that of his strong enemy Aurangzeb. Religion is the top priority for both of them. In Aurangzeb it was in the form of the pettiest and the narrowest fanaticism. He had taken birth only to become the cause of destruction. Shivaji is a godly incarnation who became the cause for victory of the Hindus and the establishment of a state."

A Great Social Reformer

Shivaji had one another face of a social reformer. Othodox people, who take Hinduism to be their property, can not tolerate inclusion into their religion of a person following any other religion, but Shivaji without caring for such orthodox people did this. Netaji Palkar and Bajaji Nimbalkar were forcibly converted into Muslims, but Shivaji turned them back into Hindus taking their consent; otherwise for them the gateway to the Hindu religion was closed forever. Unfortunately, Shivaji met with a premature death. Had he lived a little longer, he would have improved this work more. The Hindu society will remain indebted to him for this forever. Even after stiff opposition he revived the caste system based on work proving himself to be a Kshatriya by his deeds. His this deed is also a form of social reform.

Shivaji is an ideal hero of the Indian history. In fact he had all the qualities of a noble hero as mentioned in poetry. He removed the only lacking of not being a 'Kshatriya' by his noble deeds. Attracted by the virtues of this great man many Indian litterateurs have made him the topic of their writings.

One of his counterpart British traders wrote comparing him to Alexander the Great, "Shivaji is a true friend, a super enemy and very clever. He is surprisingly always victorious. The thing that Raja Shivaji has wished for is the fame of being a strong triumphant. He entered Karnataka in the same way as Caesar had entered spain for victory. He captured two strong forts, Jinji and Vellore. In this matter he is no less skilful than Alexander the Great..."

In fact Shivaji was great—Shivaji the great due to all his virtues.

www.ingramcontent.com/pod-product-compliance
Lightning Source LLC
LaVergne TN
LVHW010433230826
846092LV00009BA/1148

* 9 7 9 8 1 2 8 8 0 8 2 6 4 *